VIOLENT CRIMINAL ACTS

AND

ACTORS REVISITED

Lonnie Athens

Foreword by Herbert Blumer

University of Illinois Press   Urbana and Chicago

© 1997 by the Board of Trustees of the University of Illinois
Manufactured in the United States of America
P 5 4 3 2
This book is printed on acid-free paper.
Library of Congress Cataloging-in-Publication Data
Athens, Lonnie H.
Violent criminal acts and actors revisited / Lonnie Athens ;
foreword by Herbert Blumer.
p.   cm.
Includes bibliographical references and index.
ISBN 0-252-06608-1 (pbk. : acid-free paper)
1. Violent crimes. 2. Criminals. 3. Violence. I. Title.
HV6789.A82   1997
364.1'5—dc20   96-25235   CIP

*To my grandfather, L. D. Zaharias,
who finished only the third grade
in his native Greece but later got
his Ph.D. from the school of hard
knocks in America.*

Contents

Preface

Violent Criminal Acts and Actors was first published in 1980; since then many significant developments have taken place in the study of violent crime and in symbolic interactionism, the theoretical perspective from which I conducted the study described in this book. My initial plan was to revise the text substantially and include several new chapters. In the end I decided to present the 1980 edition as part 1 of a new book, *Violent Criminal Acts and Actors Revisited,* and to take a second look at the original study in part 2. In this way I could keep the original study relatively intact while adding new material.

Readers familiar with *Violent Criminal Acts and Actors* will notice that in this edition I use a truthful, subjective voice rather than a false, objective one; that I have added a new introductory chapter where I define and illustrate the problem under study; that I have added some new lead-in sentences and fleshed out some previously understated points (especially in chapters 4 and 7); and that I have included the rest of cases 9 (chapter 7), 24 (chapter 5), and 49 (chapter 4), omitted from the original text because of unwarranted fear that the material might be too graphic for some readers. Stylistic changes have been made throughout, and for the reader's convenience I have combined the reference lists for both parts of the book into a single bibliography. Finally, I use the masculine pronoun generically to avoid awkward, wordy prose. Thus the ensuing discussion applies to both men and women rather than to men alone. The one thing I have not changed in part 1 is my original argument.

Over the years I have received the help and encouragement of many people. Herbert Blumer offered invaluable suggestions on how to solve many of the problems encountered while conducting the original study; he also read and criticized several versions of the manuscript prior to its first publication. Marilyn O'Rourke generously typed the original manuscript, and her suggestions were incorporated throughout.

I also wish to thank the correctional institutions where the study was conducted and the University of California at Berkeley for the Chancellor's Patent Fund Award that paid for my many trips back and forth to those facilities. My deepest gratitude, however, is reserved for the subjects of this book. Their candid portraits of themselves and frank revelations of their misdeeds provided me the hard data that made this study possible.

For stimulating my early interest in criminology, I am indebted to Marshall B. Clinard, the most colorful character I've ever encountered in an institution of higher learning. While Blumer taught me the fundamentals of the interpretive approach, Clinard taught me the fundamentals of criminology. Unfortunately neither one of them taught me how to apply the fundamentals of the former to the latter.

I would also like to take this opportunity to thank a number of people who have contributed in one way or another to my efforts to become a criminologist: family members Petros, Irene, Erico, William, Heidi, and Constance Athens; the Reverend C. N. Dombalis, from my church; Joseph Page and Heathcote Wales, from the Georgetown University Law Center; Warren B. von Schuch, William W. Davenport, and Elizabeth Bernhard, from the office of the Chesterfield County Commonwealth's Attorney; and last but not least, Michael P. Markowitz, a treasured friend since grade school.

For their painstaking commentary on part 2, I am grateful to two Greek scribes, Nick and Effie Pavlou Janilus, and for his painstaking commentary on both parts 1 and 2, I am grateful to the wordsmith Bruce Bethell. Maureen Athens, my daughter, prepared the index. Norman K. Denzin, John M. Johnson, Jennifer Weatherford Athens, and Maureen Athens deserve most of the blame for the reappearance of this book in its new guise because they convinced me that *Violent Criminal Acts and Actors* could be successfully rehabilitated. Richard J. Martin, from the University of Illinois Press, deserves credit for seeing to it that I finally completed the rehabilitation process after a faculty summer research stipend from Seton Hall University provided me the impetus I needed to get started.

THE ORIGINAL STUDY

Foreword

Herbert Blumer

Sensitive and informed scholars of our contemporary social scene must be aware of the puzzling problem that is set by the occurrence and character of violent human conduct. On one hand, a growth in the extent and forms of violence seems to be taking place in conjunction with the increasing mobility of modern life. On the other hand, the steadily increasing scholarly study of violent behavior does not appear to yield much gain in the analysis and understanding of violent behavior. How is this to be explained? The lagging state of our scholarly knowledge of violent behavior is a reflection of the difficulties in isolating and studying the effective factors that are involved in violent behavior. We can appreciate this point more easily when we note that the areas in which we have succeeded in expanding our understanding represent areas or phases of violent behavior which carry some form of group endorsement or sanction. Thus, the violence that one notes today in guerrilla warfare, in political terrorism, or in gang warfare can be understood relatively easily when one considers the play of such justifying features as a sense of group mission or the feelings that are rooted in group affiliation. The genuine difficulties in analyzing and understanding violent behavior arise when one deals with violent behavior that lies outside of group endorsement and direction. Here, speaking metaphorically, violent conduct appears in a pristine form. It represents violent action that emerges outside of public sanction and in defiance of established laws and moral principles. It is the type of violent behavior which has challenged human societies since time immemorial. It is the type of violence that we are familiar with in the case of violent criminal offenders.

It may seem strange, indeed intemperate, to suggest that we are stymied in understanding violent criminal behavior. Few areas of human group life have been studied as assiduously as that of crime. The violent forms of criminal behavior, such as homicide, have been particularly the object of scientific study by many scholars over many decades. Such studies have yielded vast quantities of diversified data and have been attended by an abundance of theoretical schemes seeking to account for violent criminal behavior. Yet I think that we must candidly admit that despite the vast amount of study and the many diverse directions of theorizing, we have relatively little solid knowledge of violent criminal behavior. We get one indication of this in the confused and contradictory character of our theories and, indeed, of a great deal of our data. But more striking and important is the inability of our present criminological knowledge to offer a basis for genuinely effective control over violent criminal behavior, whether along the line of prevention or the line of correction. The record of efforts at control or elimination is dismal. We are forced to recognize that violent crime persists as a pressing and baffling problem even in our sophisticated and scientifically advanced societies.

Such an unfavorable observation immediately invites attention to the ways in which violent criminal behavior is being studied and analyzed. The failure to develop the desired body of scientific knowledge, despite the vast amount of serious study that has been undertaken, suggests that such study has not come to grips in a basic way with violent criminal behavior. It may be that a new approach is in order, one that comes closer to the detection and study of violent behavior as it actually takes place in the empirical world. This is essentially the lead that underlies the present work of Dr. Lonnie Athens. He has sought in a pioneering effort to approach the study of violent criminal behavior from the point of view that has come to be known as "symbolic interactionism."

A brief explanation of symbolic interaction may be inserted here to help understand Dr. Athens's line of study. The symbolic interactionist approach rests on the premise that human action takes place always in a situation that confronts the actor and that the actor acts on the basis of *defining this situation* that confronts him. Thus, the study of violent behavior would require that the student identify the way in which the actor sees and defines the situation in which he is placed and in which he comes to act violently. According to symbolic interactionism, the observation of human behavior in this fashion brings one's study to the very threshold of the actual empirical behavior with which one is concerned. This approach to the study of violent action is definitely different from the outstanding conventional ways that mark the field of criminology. The conventional approaches to the study of violent crime lie predominantly along two lines: (a) to seek the causes or correlates of violent crime by pursuing aggregate studies and (b) to seek such causes in the personal makeup of the individual offender. The aggregate type of study rests on the premise that violent crime is to be understood by identifying the antecedent aggregate factors with which such crime is connected. The personality type of study favors a clinical probing into personality composition for factors to explain the violence. Neither of these two conventional approaches concerns itself first and foremost with the immediate violent act or with the experience of the violent offender in the formation and execution of his act. Instead, both approaches take the violent act as a "given" without seeking to study it; they seek analysis and explanation by turning to "causative" factors that are there prior to the violent act. Consequently, for both approaches the data and their explanation stand apart, remotely apart, from the violent act in its concreteness and its immediate happening. The conventional approaches jump away from an examination of the immediate empirical act that needs to be explained, and they seek their data in areas long antecedent to and remote from the immediate empirical act. This is the reason why both of the conventional approaches fail in so many ways to explain criminal behavior, such as their inability to answer the following questions: (a) why do so many individuals not engage in violent behavior even though they have all of the characteristics of the aggregate population that is declared to have high causative or correlative relation with violent behavior; and (b) why does an offender with a constant personality makeup vary so pronouncedly in whether or not he engages in violent behavior even though the situations that confront him are objectively alike? It should be evident that the conventional study of criminal violence directs its attention elsewhere than to the action that constitutes the violence.

Dr. Athens has focused his study on the violent acts of the offender. He has worked with a sizable number of criminal violent offenders, studying them intensively. He has endeavored to have his informants describe their violent acts in a way that would allow him to identify their situations as seen by them and to trace their interpretations of these respective situations. This type of inquiry requires, admittedly, a great deal of skill and resourcefulness, such as an ability to establish good rapport with one's informants, to develop familiarity with their worlds, and to pursue flexible lines of questioning. Fortunately, Dr. Athens is well qualified in all three respects. Through several years of experience he has come to know the world and the language of violent offenders, he is resourceful in establishing rapport with them, and he has developed a high order of skill in probing into their experiences. I know of no field sociologist who is better equipped than Dr. Athens to pursue the type of inquiry described in this work.

Dr. Athens's study of the violent action of criminals is to the best of my knowledge the only such study that has been made from the standpoint of symbolic interactionism. It is truly a pioneering effort and a rewarding effort. Without any previous study to chart the way, he has had to carve out his own scheme of analysis. In my judgment, he has done this in a very commendable fashion. He has identified the major ways by which his subjects defined the situations in which they committed their violent acts; this has enabled him to devise an intriguing classification of violent offenders. He has traced the general ways by which the process of interpretation furthers or inhibits violent action. He has shown, in the true spirit of George Herbert Mead, how the formation of generalized others plays into and influences the interpretive process. And, using the knowledge derived from these lines of study, he has sought to distinguish between the different career lines of violent offenders—why some become fixed in violent behavior, why some become increasingly more violent, and why others steadily diminish their violence. All of these findings are of solid significance. They throw a great deal of light on matters that are either obscured or overlooked in conventional study. They suggest ways of exercising effective control of violent behavior. They point to lines of study that offer considerable promise of pinning down the elusive aspects of violent behavior. They make this book a very important book.

In my judgment, students in the social sciences in general and in criminology in particular will find the present work to be well worth their study and cogitation. It opens the door to a much-needed form of study in the grand task that confronts criminology.

1 The Problem: Violent Criminal Acts and Actors

According to Edwin Sutherland, America's most famous criminologist, the field of criminology has three major parts, often referred glibly to as the "three Cs of criminology": criminalization, criminality, and corrections (Sutherland and Cressey 1978, p. 3). Criminalization involves the study of the conditions under which criminal laws develop and the processes by which they are carried out. Criminality involves the study of criminal acts and the people who commit them. Finally, corrections involves the study of the practices used to treat people who have broken criminal laws.

The study described in this book falls into the second category because it focuses on the problem of *violent criminality,* that is, the acts of criminal homicide, aggravated robbery, felonious assault, and forcible rape and the individuals who commit them. The nature of this problem is vividly illustrated in the following two violent criminal acts and self-portraits of their perpetrators.

Case 25: The Act (Forcible Rape)

While I was an orderly working in the emergency room of a hospital, a young woman came in with a bad cut on her arm. She was about average in looks, but she had a better than average body with nice long, hefty legs and a nice broad ass. I showed her to one of the cubicles where patients were treated. I started a conversation with her. I asked her how she got hurt. . . . From the way that she talked and acted, I got the impression that she was a woman who made men come after her. She was conceited and all wrapped up in herself. While we were talking, I couldn't stop wondering about how she would look nude. I tried to get something going with her, but her nose was too far up in the air. She acted like she was way above me. I wanted to bone her bad, although I knew that I wasn't going to get to first base with her. While I was sitting there thinking about boning her, the doctor walked in. After he stitched her up, she split.

While at work a couple days later, she came back into my mind. I figured that I could get her name and address from the outpatient log. My pistol was in my car. I started getting excited thinking about breaking into her pad and ripping her off. When I got off work later that night, I headed straight for her pad. She lived in a first-floor apartment. When I got there, I noticed a dim light coming from one of the rooms. I crept around and looked in the window of the room where the light was coming from. I could see her lying on the floor of her bedroom with only her panties on doing some kind of exercises. Her titties were changing shape as she exercised, and I got hard. I wanted to bone her right then and there and wondered what would happen if I just tapped on her window and pointed my pistol at her. I figured that she would start screaming and someone would call the police, so I decided to wait and not break in until after she went to sleep. After she finished exercising, she grabbed some clothes and went into the bathroom. I heard the shower running and went around to the bathroom window. I couldn't see a thing, so I came back to her bedroom window and waited. When she came out of the bathroom fifteen minutes later, she flipped the lights out and jumped into bed. While I waited for her to get sound to sleep, I fantasized about tearing off her nightie and panties and boning her good.

About two or three hours later, I decided it was safe to break in. I put my mask over my face and checked all the windows. Her kitchen window was unlocked, and I climbed through it. Without making any noise, I then tiptoed into her bedroom. I was standing next to her bed staring at her, trying to get up my courage, when she suddenly woke up on her own. When she saw me, she sat up and sucked in her breath. Then I grabbed her by the shoulder, pointed my pistol between her eyes, and said, "If you make even one sound, I'll shoot you." I dug the horror that I saw start in her eyes and then spread all over her face.

I didn't want her to know that I was after her pussy because she might panic and start fighting me, so I asked her how much money she had around the pad to throw her off the track. She said, "I only have $15 in my purse." Since I wanted to get her completely helpless, I said, "Don't lie like that to me. I'm going to tie you up and search for myself." Then she swore to me that was all the money that she had and begged me not to tie her up, saying, "Please don't tie me up. Please don't . . . ," but I said, "I'm not going to take any chances with you; getting tied up is a lot better than getting your head blown off." Then I grabbed her sheet and tore it apart. I tied her hands to the bedposts. I tried to tie her feet too, but she kicked them away from me and asked, "Why are you tying me up like this?" I pointed my pistol at her head again and said, "Shut up and give me your foot."

After I tied her feet to the bedposts, I pulled the rest of the covers off her and started slowly rolling her negligee up around her neck. She started crying and said, "Please don't do that. Please don't, please. . . ." I said, "Whatever I do to you is better than you getting shot, right?" I put my hand on one of her tits and kept rubbing it over her nipple. She started crying. After I cut off her panties with my pocketknife, I pulled down my pants. I got on top of her and drove my rod all the way up her. After I stroked my dick in and out of her four or five good times, I busted my nut. Then I got off her and wiped my dick off with her bedspread. Although it was all over in about a minute, she kept sobbing away. I told her that I was going to search the place for money and that she better not move. I went into the living room and then quietly split out the front door.

Case 25: The Actor

I was a lover and a fighter, not any more one than the other. I did wild things, like bar hopping, taking drugs, getting into fights, and looking for some strange on the side. My wife and younger brother thought that I was a real handsome and tough dude who could kick men's asses and get plenty of women, too. They also thought that I was mean because of my bad temper and the cruelty that I could inflict on people if they ever crossed me. I had a tough-guy attitude and played hard. I could hurt people both mentally and physically. Although I was definitely cold-blooded, I think that they saw me as a lot badder than I really was. I would fuck up a man or woman real bad, but I wasn't a killer. I couldn't kill anybody unless my back was against the wall.

My wife didn't trust me around other women for a minute because she knew that I wanted to fuck a lot of different broads. I often wouldn't fuck her until she begged me for it. I would tell her to go out and sell her pussy to the highest bidder or fuck anybody that she wanted. I would also check out other broads right in front of her and make remarks about their bodies. She called me an exhibitionist because when I went out, I liked to show off my long rod. I wouldn't wear any underwear and would jack my pants up real high so broads could see my rod. Then I'd start small talk with them and would act like I just wanted to make their acquaintance when all I was really thinking about was boning them. I would bone anything that wore a skirt.

What I really needed was some freaky sex. Other guys got it, and I wanted it too. When I was a kid, I got a big kick out of sneaking peeks through the keyhole at my stepmother's big hairy bush, but afterwards I felt like I couldn't look her straight in the eyes. My secret desire was to have threesomes with my wife, go to orgies, and watch lesbians get down and other people fuck. I plain and simple needed to get some good, hot, kinky sex but resented having to rely on the generosity of women to hit on their pussies. My days of begging a bitch for the pleasure of touching her pussy were over. I would still be nice to women, but if they resisted my advances, then I would rip them off for some pussy.

Case 55: The Act (Criminal Homicide)

A partner of mine said he might come over to my pad with some broads, so I hurried over to the liquor store right around the corner to get a case of beer. As I was walking across the parking lot of the store, this guy almost ran me over. I flipped him off. The driver and his partners jumped out of the car and rat-packed me. They knocked me down, and the driver pushed my head into the dirt next to the cigarette butts. Then they went into the store. I just felt, "What a low fucking thing to do to somebody. They are just a bunch of yellow motherfuckers." In my mind I suddenly thought, "I've got to get back at these dirty motherfuckers," and I ran back to my pad for my rifle.

I got back to the liquor store as fast as I possibly could and waited for them about twenty yards from the front door of the store. While I was waiting, I kept trying to decide whether I should shoot to wound the motherfuckers or kill them, and whether I should shoot only the driver or his partners too. Finally his two partners popped out the door. I said to myself, "Fuck it, I'll shoot all of them." I fired two quick, wild shots but missed them both, and they got away. I decided then that I better put the barrel to the chest of the motherfucker who I really wanted—the driver—and make sure that I didn't miss him. I had stone hatred for him, and I righteously couldn't wait to see the look on his face when I blew him away. As soon as he popped out of the liquor store door, I charged right up to him, rammed the barrel in his chest, and pulled the trigger.

Case 55: The Actor

I was a burned-out low rider, but I still didn't want any part of the square program. I had quit the school scene, messed up in the service, and never dug the eight-hour-a-day job shit. My old lady and family thought that I had become a for-real fuckup and had turned into a lousy fool, but I didn't care what they thought. All that I cared about was taking drugs. I was a full-fledged dope fiend who was righteously hooked. I only hung out with other thieves who, like me, were mainliners, pill chewers, and stoneheads. Although I had good connections, I had to worry every day about getting enough money to score. When I was hurting bad, I would rip people off to get money for drugs.

My family and neighbors were scared to death of me. They knew that I was hotheaded, full of hate, and could do any fucking thing to somebody. When I came around, they treated me like the walking dead. Even young up-and-coming low riders acted leery of me. If somebody fucked with me, I would righteously blow them away. I was a flipped-out dope fiend who was subject to kill or do worse to people. I would get down with anything—fists, knives, broken bottles, pistols, rifles, sawed-off shotguns. I could kill or fuck up somebody bad without losing any sleep over it, but I still think the great fear that people had of me was somewhat exaggerated. They acted like I was some kind of mass murderer, serial killer, or something.

Criminologists have long ballyhooed their study of criminality as being scientific (Sellin 1938, p. 4). Any field of study that touts itself as a science must operate on certain minimal assumptions. The first and foremost assumption is that there is a world "out there," beyond the scientists, that they can study. The impossibility of studying this empirical world with a "blank mind" is the second assumption. Scientists always study the empirical world with certain notions, however well thought-out, already in their minds. The third assumption is that the empirical world can resist the scientist's approach or preconceived ideas about it. When the empirical world "talks back" to scientists in this way, they must be willing to revise or discard the approach with which they have been studying it (Blumer 1969, pp. 21–40). As the radical empiricist Herbert Blumer (1969) admonishes, scientists must always "respect the nature of the empirical world under study" and "organize a methodological stance to reflect that respect" (p. 60).

In the next chapter I examine the scientific approaches that criminologists have typically adopted in the study of violent criminality. While reviewing these standard approaches, I repeatedly raise the same question: do *concrete instances of violent criminal acts and actors,* such as those previously described in cases 25 and 55, resist explanation under these approaches? If we conclude that none of the standard scientific approaches can overcome the resistance that actual violent criminal acts and actors present to them, and we take seriously the claim that the study of violent criminality is scientific, then criminologists have no choice. No matter how intellectually distasteful it may be, they must discard all their standard approaches and search for a new, scientific approach to take in the study of this old but still troubling problem. In short, they must find an approach to the study of violent criminality that is much more faithful to the *actual* nature of human action and actors and that thereby respects far better the empirical world of violent crime in its true, ugly reality.

2 A Review and Critique of the Dominant Approaches Taken in the Study of Violent Criminality

Over the last thirty years three distinct approaches have dominated the study of violent criminality: the aggregate-characteristic approach, the personality approach, and the interdisciplinary approach. The assumptions on which each of these approaches rest will be elucidated and an exemplar of each will be provided.

AGGREGATE-CHARACTERISTIC APPROACH

The aggregate-characteristic approach is based on the assumption that the causes of violent crime will be revealed from statistical uniformities in the "material" characteristics of violent offenses, offenders, and their victims supplied in official sources of information, such as police reports. Hypotheses that uniformities or statistical patterns exist in these characteristics are implicitly or explicitly tested. Most studies done from this approach investigate the material characteristics of just one type of violent crime. Researchers thus search for uniformities in the material characteristics of criminal homicide, armed robbery, aggravated assault, or forcible rape rather than for uniformities of violent crime in general.[1]

David Pittman and William Handy's 1964 study of aggravated assault in St. Louis provides one of the best examples of this approach. According to Pittman and Handy, "the purpose of this study is to analyze the crime of aggravated assault and to establish its 'patterns'" (p. 462). To accomplish this purpose, they examined 241, or a 25 percent random sample, of the 965 crimes classified as aggravated assault by the St. Louis Metropolitan Police Department over a one-year period. Data were gathered from police reports filed on these crimes and from arrest records of the offenders and victims. Analyzing these data, Pittman and Handy tested hypotheses about the time and location of the offenses, the season of the year when they were committed, the type of weapons used by the offenders, the involvement of alcohol in the offenses, the relationship of offenders to victims, and the previous arrest records of the offenders and victims.

Reasoning that "during weekdays interaction among people is limited by their work, and there is less leisure time than on the weekends," Pittman and Handy hypothesized that "the majority of the acts of aggravated assault would occur between 6:00 P.M. Friday and 6:00 A.M. Monday." This hypothesis was confirmed, with 132 of the 241 offenses occurring during the stated time period. They further hypothesized that "the majority of the acts would occur between 8:00 P.M. on a given evening and 4:00 A.M. the following morning." This hypothesis was also confirmed, with 140 of the offenses occurring between 8:00 P.M. and 4:00 A.M. (p. 463).

Pittman and Handy made several hypotheses about the place and time of year in which the offenses would occur. They first hypothesized that "the largest number of acts would occur on public streets rather than in taverns or bars, residences or other places." This hypothesis was confirmed, with 110 of the 241 offenses taking place on public streets, 91 in residences, and only 27 in taverns or bars. With respect to season, their hypothesis was that more violent acts would be committed during the winter than during other seasons. Since 87 of the offenses occurred during the summer months and 82 during the winter months, this hypothesis was rejected. Considering the influence of season on the location of the offense, they then hypothesized that "during the winter months, a greater number of acts would occur indoors as against the summer, when the larger number would occur outdoors." This hypothesis was also rejected since the number of offenses occurring indoors and outdoors was almost identical in the winter and in the summer (p. 464).

With respect to the weapon used in the offense, Pittman and Handy hypothesized that "a knife, being readily accessible, would be used in more instances than any other weapon." They found that a knife was used in 126 of the 241 cases, a gun in 39, and personal force in 14, thereby confirming the hypothesis. On the basis of their assumption "that in Negro neighborhoods weapons for self defense are commonly carried," they further hypothesized that "proportionately, white offenders would use personal force to a greater extent than would Negro offenders." This hypothesis was also confirmed, with white offenders using personal force significantly more often than black offenders did. Finally, they hypothesized that "prior alcohol ingestion by both the offender and victim would be common in acts of aggravated assault." This hypothesis was not confirmed, however. The ingestion of alcohol was found to be present in only slightly more than one-quarter of the cases (pp. 464–67).

Regarding the relationship between the offender and victim, Pittman and Handy tested several hypotheses. After finding that the victims and offenders were of the same race in 228 of the 238 cases in which the races of both parties had been ascertained, they reasoned that "if the offender and victim were of the same race, they would be of the same sex." Their data also supported this hypothesis, because the sexes of the victim and offender were the same in 144 of the 238 cases in which the sexes were known. On the assumption that "persons of the same age are most likely to interact with one another," they then hypothesized that "the victim and offender would be within the same age category." This hypothesis was supported by the data, with 146 of the 241 cases involving offenders falling within the same age groups (p. 467).

Pittman and Handy also tested the hypothesis that the offenders' prior arrest records would differ from the victims'. Their hypothesis was confirmed. A significant difference was found in the frequency with which offenders and victims had previously been arrested: 156 of the 248 offenders had prior arrest records, whereas only 121 of the 252 victims did. Moreover, 37 of the offenders with prior records had been previously arrested at least once for assault. Lastly, they hypothesized that "Negro offenders would be no more likely to have prior arrest records than white offenders; this belief was confirmed" (p. 468).

From their tests of these hypotheses about the material characteristics of this offense, Pittman and Handy concluded that "it is possible to state the expected pattern of aggravated assault in the 'typical' case" (p. 469). They describe the typical case in the following manner:

> An act of aggravated assault is more likely to occur on a weekend than during the week, specifically between 6:00 P.M. Friday and 6:00 A.M. Monday. . . . While the event shows little likelihood of being more frequent in the four summer months considered together than in the winter, this type of assault peaks in the months of July and August. . . .
>
> The crime will occur on a public street, or, secondly, in a residence. . . .
>
> The weapon used by both men and women will in most cases be a knife, with a gun the second choice. . . .

These records indicate that neither the offender nor the victim will be under the influence of alcohol. . . .

The offender and victim will be of the same race and of the same sex. . . . Both will be of the same age group. . . .

Negro offenders are no more likely than their white counterparts to have a prior arrest record. (p. 469)

PERSONALITY APPROACH

The personality approach is based on the assumption that abnormal personality makeups cause people to commit violent crimes. Thus hypotheses that link certain personality traits to violent criminal behavior are implicitly or explicitly tested.[2] Various kinds of psychological tests are administered to violent and nonviolent offenders to determine whether any personality trait or constellation of traits differentiates them. Undoubtedly Edwin Megargee (1966) has provided the most sophisticated example of this approach.

Megargee hypothesized that an individual who commits a violent crime almost always has one of two types of personalities. One type is called an undercontrolled personality; the other, an overcontrolled personality. Both are viewed as abnormal since they deviate from the normal personality in their level of self-control or inhibitions against aggression. With respect to a person with an undercontrolled personality, Megargee contends: "The Undercontrolled Aggressive person corresponds to the typical conception of an aggressive personality. . . . He is a person whose inhibitions against aggressive behavior are quite low. Consequently, he usually responds with aggression whenever he is frustrated or provoked" (p. 2). And with respect to a person with an overcontrolled personality, he states:

> The Chronically Overcontrolled type behaves quite differently, however. His inhibitions against the expression of aggression are extremely rigid so he rarely, if ever, responds with aggression no matter how great the provocation. . . . The result is that through some form of temporal summation . . . his instigation to aggression builds up over time. In some cases, the instigation to aggression summates to the point where it exceeds even his excessive defenses. If this occurs when there are sufficient cues to aggression in the environment, an aggressive act should result. (pp. 2–3)

There is an important difference between the aggressive behavior of persons with undercontrolled personalities and that of persons with over-controlled personalities. The difference lies in the nature of the relation-ships among: (1) the provocation or the immediate frustrating stimulus, (2) the instigation or drive to aggression, and (3) the resulting overt response. In the case of the undercontrolled person, these factors are directly pro-portional to one another. A greater provocation produces a stronger drive to aggression and a more aggressive overt response (Megargee 1973, p. 39). In the case of the overcontrolled person, however, these are usually dis-proportional to one another. Once his drive to aggression has summated, or built up over time, to a point that reaches his level of self-control, the overcontrolled person makes an aggressive response of lethal intensity, even if he is only slightly provoked (Megargee 1966, p. 22, 1973, p. 39). Thus Megargee (1966) reasons that "the former may commit aggressive responses of any intensity depending upon the immediate stimulus situa-tion, while the latter tends to inhibit aggressive responses until they break through in . . . an extremely assaultive response in which the very life of the victim may be jeopardized" (p. 17).

Megargee (1965) invokes an analogy to describe persons with these two types of abnormal personalities:

Suppose we regard a man's inhibitions against aggression as a dam, and his impulses to aggression as the water which seeks to flow past. Whenever the water rises above the top of the dam, it spills over into the valley below, causing disturbance—but not nearly as much as if the dam suddenly collapsed in a rain storm and let go all at once. The undercontrolled aggressive person . . . has inhibitions which are like a low or incomplete dam. Very little water is blocked, and very little backs up. . . . Almost any provocation results in aggression, and the amount of aggression will be determined by the amount of provocation. . . . The people downstream from him may, therefore, be in constant discomfort and apprehension and clamor for more protection.

The chronically overcontrolled type, however, is very different. His dam is both too high and too rigid. There is no "water over the dam" which can be discharged and forgotten; no emergency bypasses or spillways. Not a drop gets through, and the people downstream are dry, and careless, and perhaps even contemptuous. The thought of disaster never occurs to them. But the pressure builds up and up, and must finally have a vent. Since the structure was not built to handle major strains, one drop too many may cause a complete rupture and release the pent-up fury all at once. And so explodes the unexpected crime of violence.

Megargee has conducted the most comprehensive study testing the under- and overcontrolled personality hypothesis. The rationale behind his study (Megargee 1966) is that a sample of people who have committed extremely assaultive acts should contain both over- and undercontrolled individuals, whereas a sample of people who have committed moderately assaultive acts should contain only undercontrolled individuals. According to Megargee, "On various indexes or measures of aggressiveness and control, then, the extremely assaultive group should appear less aggressive and more controlled *as a group* than would either the moderately aggressive group or a nonassaultive sample" (p. 3).

Seventy-six male delinquents who were detained in a county juvenile hall for various offenses were selected as subjects. The subjects were divided into the following four groups: nine boys who had committed extremely assaultive offenses (EA group), twenty-one boys who had committed moderately assaultive offenses (MA group), twenty boys who were detained only for incorrigibility (I group), and twenty-six boys who had committed property offenses only (PO group). The I and PO groups were matched with the assaultive groups on age, race, and number of prior detentions (pp. 6–7).

Data were collected on the subjects' predetention behavior, detention behavior, and personality makeup. The data on predetention behavior were taken from probation officers' reports. Analysis of these data resulted in several findings. The more important ones include the following: (1) the EA group had significantly fewer previous detentions than did the MA group, (2) the EA group had satisfactory school attendance records significantly more often than did the other groups, and (3) the EA group had satisfactory school conduct records somewhat more often than did the other groups (pp. 9–10).

Data on the behavior of the subjects during their detention in juvenile hall were obtained by means of an aggressive-behavior checklist, a favorable-behavior rating scale, and an overcontrolled-behavior index derived from the Gough Adjective Checklist. Among the more important findings are the following: (1) the EA group had insignificantly lower verbal and physical aggression scores on the behavior checklist than did the other groups, (2) the EA group had an insignificantly higher score on the favorable-behavior scale than did the other groups, and (3) the EA group had a significantly higher score on the overcontrolled-behavior index than did the other groups (p. 13).

Finally, the data on the subjects' personality traits were provided by a battery of psychological tests: the California Personality Inventory (CPI), the Rosenzweig Picture-Frustration Test (P-F), the Thematic Apperception Test (TAT), and the Holtzman Inkblot Test (HIT). Among the more important findings resulting from the analysis of these test data are the following: (1) the EA group had an insignificantly higher self-control score on the CPI than did the other groups, (2) the EA group had a lower extrapunitive score on the P-F than did the MA group but had a higher one than did the I or P groups, (3) the EA group displayed a lower need aggression score on the TAT than did the PO or I groups but a higher one than the MA group, and (4) the EA group also displayed the highest hostility score on the HIT of all the groups' (pp. 14–17).

On the basis of his analysis of the predetention behavior, detention behavior, and personality traits of these four groups, Megargee concluded that "the results were by no means unequivocal in their support for the hypothesis. Nevertheless, by and large, a review of the data indicates consistent if not spectacular support for the writer's hypothesis" (pp. 17–18). With respect to the generally negative findings produced by the psychological tests, he rationalizes that "it is not too surprising that the behavior on the psychological tests is not as clear-cut as that observed in detention or found in the case history. Studies . . . have demonstrated the greater validity of case history as opposed to psychological tests. This tendency to find greater clarity in direct measures as opposed to tests would probably be accentuated in a correctional setting such as the one in which these data were collected" (p. 17).

INTERDISCIPLINARY APPROACH

The interdisciplinary approach is based on the assumption that people commit violent crimes because of a confluence of factors traditionally studied in more than one discipline rather than in a single one. Moreover these divergent factors are assumed to be causally connected, although the exact nature of this connection may not be specified. Thus researchers espousing this view formulate and test hypotheses that link in one causal chain factors that are usually studied in different disciplines. Marvin Wolfgang, a sociologist, and Franco Ferracuti, a psychologist, offer the premier illustration of this approach to violent criminality.[3]

Combining the factors of subculture and social class from sociology with that of personality from psychology, Wolfgang and Ferracuti hypothesize that "overt (and often illicit) expression of violence (of which homicide is only the most extreme) is part of a subcultural normative system and that this system is reflected in the psychological traits of the subcultural participants" (Wolfgang and Ferracuti 1964, p. 294, 1967a, p. 158). According to these writers, this subcultural normative system is localized within the lower social class of a society (Ferracuti and Wolfgang 1963, pp. 379–81, 1964, p. 293; Wolfgang 1967, p. 11).

To further fill out their hypothesis, Wolfgang and Ferracuti add seven corollary propositions:

1. No subculture can be totally different from or totally in conflict with the society of which it is a part.
2. To establish the existence of a subculture of violence does not require that all persons sharing in this basic value element express violence in all situations.
3. The ubiquitous presence of potential resort to violence in a variety of situations emphasizes the penetrating and diffuse nature of this cultural theme.
4. The subcultural ethos of violence may be shared by all ages in a subsociety, but this ethos is most prominent in a limited age group ranging from late adolescence to middle age.
5. The counter-norm is nonviolence.
6. The development of favorable attitudes toward and the use of violence in this subculture usually involve learned behavior and a process of differential learning, association, or identification.
7. The use of violence in a subculture is not necessarily viewed as illicit behavior, and the users therefore do not have to deal with feelings of guilt about their aggression. (Ferracuti and Wolfgang 1964, pp. 294–98; Wolfgang and Ferracuti 1967a, pp. 158–61)

Wolfgang and Ferracuti qualify this hypothesis by making a distinction between "idiopathic" and "normatively prescribed" violent crimes. Idiopathic violent crimes are committed by people who suffer from some major psychopathology, whereas normatively prescribed ones are committed by people who are members of a subculture of violence. The former individuals are usually from the middle or upper social classes, whereas the latter are from the lower social class. The subculture of violence hypothesis does not, of course, apply to idiopathic violent crimes. Wolfgang and Ferracuti estimate that fewer than 10 percent of violent crimes are idiopathic and thereby imply that the hypothesis has wide application to the problem of violent crime (see Ferracuti and Wolfgang 1963, pp. 378, 381–82; Wolfgang 1967, pp. 6–7; Wolfgang and Ferracuti, 1967a, pp. 140–41, 262–63, 1967b, pp. 272–73).

With Wolfgang's aid Ferracuti and Lazzari (1970) conducted the most intriguing study testing the subculture of violence hypothesis. The authors state that the purpose of their study is "to examine the subculture of violence thesis as a possible explanation for the high rates of violent crimes in specific cultures and for the proneness towards the use of violence as a problem-solving mechanism" (p. 97). Since Sardinia has a violent social code known as the "vendetta barbaricina," as well as a higher rate of violent crime than that of other regions of Italy, they (pp. 10–11, 97) designed a study to compare Sardinian and non-Sardinian violent and nonviolent offenders. The rationale behind the study was that the Sardinian violent offenders should be members of a violent subculture and thus should be distinguishable from the other offenders in the ways prescribed by the subculture of violence hypothesis (pp. 87–88, 97).

Four groups of offenders constituted the subjects for the study: thirty violent and twenty-six nonviolent offenders from Sardinia and thirty violent and thirty nonviolent offenders from other regions of Italy. These offenders were selected from the records of an observation center where males between the ages of eighteen and twenty-five are sent for clinical examination and correctional classification. Data were drawn from the offenders' files, which contained information on their offenses and on their social and family backgrounds, as well as the results of psychological tests and a psychiatric examination given to them (pp. 98–99).

Although the analysis of these data resulted in numerous findings, I will mention only those that bear most directly on the subculture of violence hypothesis. These findings resulted from comparisons between the Sardinian and non-Sardinian violent offenders and between the Sardinian violent and nonviolent offenders. The following are the most important findings resulting from the first comparison: (1) The violent Sardinians committed cruel violent crimes significantly more often than did violent non-Sardinians (p. 139). (2) The violent Sardinians committed violent crimes against family members significantly less often than did the violent non-Sardinians (142). (3) The violent Sardinians had significantly lower

FC and significantly higher S scores on the Rorschach test than did violent non-Sardinians (pp. 144, 146). (4) Violent Sardinians, however, did not significantly differ from violent non-Sardinians in aggressive scores on the TAT, Make a Picture Story Test (MAPS), or Palo Alto Scale (pp. 108–9). (5) Finally, violent Sardinians suffered from major psychiatric disturbances somewhat less often than did violent non-Sardinians (p. 71).

The following are the most important findings yielded by the comparison between violent and nonviolent Sardinian offenders: (1) The violent Sardinians had a lower educational level significantly more often than did the nonviolent Sardinians (p. 127). (2) Violent Sardinians had significantly lower FC and significantly higher CF and S scores on the Rorschach test than did the nonviolent Sardinians (pp. 144–46). (3) Violent Sardinians, however, did not significantly differ from nonviolent Sardinians in aggressive scores on the TAT, MAPS, or Palo Alto Scale (p. 109). (4) Finally, the violent Sardinians suffered from a major psychiatric disturbance significantly less often than did nonviolent Sardinians (p. 71).

From these findings Ferracuti, Lazzari, and Wolfgang concluded that the Sardinian violent offenders were indeed different from the other offenders. "Although these differences are not always clearcut such as to allow a sharp differentiation or a predictability of violent behavior," the authors state that "they are all in the same theoretical direction and in agreement with the subculture of violence hypothesis" (109). The authors specifically point out here that the Sardinian violent offenders "are more explosive, more hostile, and their crimes are committed with more cruelty" (109) and that they less often exhibit psychopathology. With regard to their negative findings on the TAT, MAPS, and Palo Alto Scale, however, they remark glibly that "the failure of the psychological tests to differentiate our groups both in thematic data and in the Palo Alto Scale is not entirely unexpected. . . . Other tests . . . might yield other results, but the semantics of violence, as expressed in phantasy themes, and other cultural variants may render cross-cultural use difficult or impossible" (110).

CRITIQUE OF THE DOMINANT APPROACHES

As in the case of most approaches taken in the study of criminality, the three just illustrated are based on positivism (see Jeffery 1960; Matza 1964, pp. 1–32; Vold 1958, pp. 27–40; Taylor, Walton, and Young 1973, p. 146). Positivism is a philosophy of science that advocates the application of the logic and methods of the physical sciences to the social and psychological sciences. It rests on the fundamental assumption that there is no essential difference between studying human beings and studying physical molecules (Schutz 1954). Although human beings may seem to possess the power of interpretation, antecedent factors are equally responsible for the reactions of molecules and those of humans. The study of all forms of human action, including criminal action, thus can be reduced to the examination of various forms of behavior—that is, overt conduct, such as killing, raping, or robbing—and their possible causes or antecedent factors.

The dominant approaches taken in the study of violent criminality are clearly positivistic. In the case of the aggregate-characteristic approach, the assumption is that the antecedent factors that cause violent criminal behavior will be revealed by studying the statistical distribution of the material characteristics of violent offenses, offenders, and victims. Thus findings are provided only on the patterns or statistical uniformities in the superficial artifacts of violent criminality. In the personality approach the assumption is that the antecedent factor is an abnormal personality, and thus findings are provided only on the personality traits of violent offenders or their presumed correlates. Finally, in the interdisciplinary approach the assumption is that the antecedent factors causing violent criminality stem from multiple, connected sources. Thus, findings are provided only on possible causal chains more diversified than those usually investigated in most studies of violent offenders.

Despite the differences among them, all positivistic approaches suffer from two serious shortcomings. First, they ignore the fact that human action is *situated:* it always takes place within a context or situation that must be *interpreted* by the person who is confronted with the situation (see Deutscher 1970). In his identification of the two primary conditions of human action, Blumer (1962) refers to this situatedness:

> One primary condition is that action takes place in and with regard to a situation . . . any particular action is formed in the light of the situation in which it takes place. This leads to the recognition of a second major condition, namely, that the action is formed or constructed by interpreting the situation. The acting unit necessarily has to identify the things which it has to take into account—tasks, opportunities, obstacles, means, demands, discomforts, dangers, and the like; it has to assess them in some fashion and it has to make decisions on the basis of the assessment. (p. 187)

In other words, human beings construct or form their actions vis-à-vis situations. They interpret situations by defining what confronts them and judging how they should handle it. On the basis of their interpretations, they carry out different courses of action in those situations.

To say that human action is situated does not imply that antecedent factors play no part in human action, however. Insofar as they enter into a person's interpretation of a situation, antecedent factors play a significant part in his action. Nevertheless the study of antecedent factors or their indicators or correlates *cannot* be substituted for the study of the interpretations in which the antecedent factors are presumed to operate; their part in the interpretation of situations can be ascertained only through the study of the interpretive process. The nature of the interpretation of the situation through which some given type of human action is constructed cannot be taken for granted. Since interpretations of situations are *creative or formative processes in their own right,* and not simply products of antecedent factors, they must always be made a special object of analysis in the study of human action. Blumer (1969) makes this point:

> We must recognize that the activity of human beings consists of meeting a flow of situations in which they have to act and that their action is built on the basis of what they note, how they assess . . . what they note, and what kind of projected lines of action they map out. This process is not caught by ascribing action to some kind of factor (for example, motives, need dispositions, role requirements, social expectations, or social rules) that is thought to initiate the action and propel it to its conclusion; such a factor, or some expression of it, is a matter the human actor takes into account in mapping his line of action. The initiating factor does not embrace or explain how it and other matters are taken into account in the situation that calls for action. One has to get inside of the defining process of the actor in order to understand his action. (p. 16)

A second shortcoming of positivistic approaches follows from the first one. In assuming that human action is determined exclusively by antecedent factors, such approaches treat the human being as merely a neutral medium through which the given antecedent factors come to expression. Positivistic approaches thereby operate on a model of human beings as *passive agents* who play no part in the formation of their actions. But human beings construct or form their actions through an interpretive process that, as just noted, is not determined solely by antecedent factors. Thus the proper model of human beings is one that sees them as *acting units,* or *actors,* who organize their actions to fit the situations that confront them. With respect to these two different models of the human being, Blumer (1969) states:

> The dominant prevailing view sees the human being as a complex organism whose behavior is a response to factors playing on the organization of the organism. Schools of thought in the social and psychological sciences differ enormously in which of such factors they regard as significant, as is shown in such a diverse array as stimuli, organic drives, need-dispositions, conscious motives, unconscious motives, emotions, attitudes, ideas, cultural prescriptions, norms, values, status demands, social roles, reference group affiliations, and institutional pressures. . . . Nevertheless, these schools of thought are alike in seeing the human being as a responding organism, with its behavior being a product of the factors playing on its organization or an expression of the interplay of parts of its organization. (p. 14)

Nonetheless he adds that the human being is "not a mere responding organism but an acting organism—an organism that has to mold a line of action on the basis of what it takes into account instead of merely releasing a response to the play of some factor on its organization" (p. 15).

By their very design, however, positivistic approaches are unable to account for human action as situated and human beings as acting units (see Blumer 1969, pp. 55–57, 132–39). As previously noted, these approaches reduce the study of human action to the empirical examination of antecedent factors or their indicators or correlates and their end product—overt conduct. Studies based on such approaches ignore individuals' interpretations of the situations in which they act and as a result completely omit the part that human beings play in the organization of their actions. Thus no empirical findings are provided on the process by which individuals interpret a situation as calling for a certain course of action on their part and then carry out that course of action. Yet without detailed knowledge of the interpretive process, human action cannot be adequately explained.

Given the limitations of positivistic approaches, we need to take a different type of approach in the study of violent criminality. What is needed is an *interpretive* approach, that is, an approach that is based on the recognition that violent criminal action is *situated* and that operates on a model of the violent criminal as an *actor*.[4] The primary requirement of such an approach is that the viewpoint of the person whose actions are under study always be explicitly taken into account in explaining his conduct (see Cooley 1926; Hayek 1952; Schutz 1954; Winch 1958; Znaniecki 1968, pp. 34–89). Blumer (1969) states the necessity for doing this as follows: "Since action is forged by the actor out of what he perceives, interprets, and judges, one would have to see the operating situation as the actor sees it, perceive objects as the actor perceives them, ascertain their meaning in terms of the meaning they have for the actor, and follow the actor's line of conduct as the actor organizes it—in short, one would have to take the role of the actor and see his world from his standpoint" (pp. 73–74).

The study that follows takes an interpretive approach to the problem of violent criminality. The exact nature of this interpretive approach is described in the next chapter.

NOTES

1. Studies done from the aggregate-characteristic approach on other violent crimes include Amir 1971; Bensing and Schroeder 1960; Chappell and Singer 1977; Curtis 1974; Driver 1961; Harlan 1950; Hepburn and Voss 1970; Landua, Drapkin, and Arad 1974; Levy, Kunitz, and Everett 1969; MacDonald 1971; Mulvihill, Tumin, and Curtis 1969; Pokorny 1965a, 1965b; Svalastoga 1962, 1956; Voss and Hepburn 1968; Wallace 1964; and Wolfgang 1958. For a critique of approaches that, like the aggregate-characteristic one, rely on official information for their source of data, see Kitsuse and Cicourel 1963.

2. Recent studies on violent criminality done from the personality approach include Carrol and Fuller 1971; Fisher and Rivlin 1971; Fisher 1970; Justice and Birkman 1972; Lester, Perdue, and Brookhart 1974; Lester and Perdue 1973; Mallory and Walker 1972; McCreary 1976; Megargee, Cook, and Mendelsohn 1967; Megargee and Cook 1967; Megargee and Mendelsohn 1962; Persons and Marks 1971; Perdue and Lester 1974, 1972; Rader 1977; Rawlings 1973; Sarbin, Wenk, and Sherwood 1968; Sarbin and Wenk 1969; Wagner and Hawkins 1964; Warder 1969; and Wenk, Sarbin, and Sherwood 1968. For a critique of the use of this approach in the study of criminality, see Sutherland and Cressy 1978, pp. 156–77.

3. They have discussed their application of this approach to the problem of violent criminality in a variety of places. See Ferracuti and Newman 1974; Ferracuti and Wolfgang 1964, 1963; Wolfgang 1968, 1967; and Wolfgang and Ferracuti 1967a, 1967b. For other related studies of violent criminality done from the interdisciplinary approach, see Ball-Rokeach 1973; Erlanger 1974; and Ferracuti and Wolfgang 1973.

4. Although most studies of criminality and deviance are done from positivistic approaches, there have been some notable exceptions done from interpretive approaches. These include the studies done by Becker on marijuana use (1953), Cressey on the violation of financial trust (1953), and Lindesmith on opiate addiction (1968). Douglas (1967) has provided an excellent, lengthy argument of the need for taking an interpretive approach in the study of suicide.

3 An Interpretive Approach

From poring over the ideas of his mentor, George Herbert Mead (1964, 1936, 1934, 1932), Herbert Blumer (1975, 1969, 1962, 1937, 1929) developed an interpretive approach to human conduct with a distinctive American flavor. In developing this approach, he made the self the pivotal notion. According to Blumer (1962, p. 181), the self has two basic, but closely connected aspects—the self as *process* and as *object.*

The first aspect, the self as process, refers to the conversations that human beings carry on continuously with themselves during their wakeful hours.[1] They carry on these self-conversations by making indications to themselves and then responding to their indications by making further self-indications. Self-indications are made whenever people note or point out anything to themselves or other people.

The process of making self-indications or conversing with oneself has four essential features. (1) People make indications to themselves *as if* they were making them to someone else, except that they make them in a *shorthand,* a more abbreviated and rapid manner. (2) When people make an indication to someone else, they always are simultaneously making an indication to themselves, although the converse may not always be true. (3) When people indicate some raw feeling or naked sensation to themselves, they transform it into a full-blown emotion. (4) When making indications to themselves or someone else, people always assume the attitude either of another person, a small discrete group of persons, or a generalized other.

By conversing with himself in this way, an individual constructs interpretations of the situations that confront him. Interpretations of a situation have two ongoing and correlated phases. The first phase is *definition.* Here the individual defines the situation facing him. He does this by assuming the attitude or attitudes of the other people in the situation and indicating to himself the meaning of the gestures that they are making toward him. Thus an individual defines the situation primarily in terms of what he sees is being done or is likely to be done by the other participants in the situation.

The second phase in interpreting the situation is *judgment*. Here the individual decides on the proper course of action to take in the situation given his definition of it. He judges the situation by assuming an attitude of his *generalized other* and indicating to himself how he ought to act. The generalized other is the *composite* attitude of the corporal community in which the individual lives. He develops it from his interaction with other people who inhabit that same community. The particular attitude of the generalized other that the individual assumes in judging a situation depends on his definition of the situation. By assuming an attitude of his generalized other, the individual forms a "plan of action" to carry out in the situation; that is, he covertly organizes or prepares himself to follow a particular course of overt action.

After the individual has judged the situation before him, however, he still may not carry out the resultant plan of action. He can always *redefine* the situation confronting him before carrying out this plan—for example, if he notes that the other participants have altered their previous courses of action. If the individual forms a new definition of the situation, then he may *rejudge* it by again assuming an attitude of his generalized other and indicating to himself how he should *now* respond to the situation. As a result he may form a *new* plan of action. Thus, once formed, a plan of action can always be dropped and replaced by another (Blumer 1969, pp. 55, 73, 96).

The second aspect of the self, the self as object, refers to the conception or picture that a human being has of himself, which is his *self-image.* An individual develops a self-image by looking at himself and then judging what he sees. He can neither see nor judge himself directly but can do so only indirectly, from a standpoint outside himself. The only way that an individual can see and judge himself from the outside is by assuming the attitudes of others and addressing himself from their positions. First he assumes the attitudes of selected persons, such as his spouse or best friend, or of small discrete groups, such as his family, clique, or gang, and looks at himself from their positions. The attitudes that they hold toward him are based on how they interpret his actions, so that to them "he is how he acts." The actor then assumes the various attitudes that constitute his generalized other, and from these different positions he judges the particular ways in which such persons and groups view him. By judging their views of him from the different attitudes of his generalized other, he forms an image of himself as this or that kind of person (see Mead 1934, pp. 138, 309; Blumer 1969, pp. 12–13).

The generalized other connects the two aspects of the self, as process and as object, because it enters both into people's interpretations of situations and into their self-images. The individual judges the situations confronting him and the attitudes that others have toward him from the positions of his generalized other.[2] Thus the image that he holds of himself is usually congruent or *in line* with the interpretations of situations that he forms. Since the generalized other is mutable, it may change over time. As it changes, the individual will begin to judge both situations and himself differently, then engage in new forms of conduct, and eventually develop a new self-image.

DESCRIPTION OF THE STUDY

In the study discussed in this book, I applied the ideas from the approach just described to the problem of violent criminality. It was thus necessary for me to collect and analyze data on the interpretations that people made of situations in which they committed violent criminal acts, the interpretations they made of situations in which they almost committed such acts, the self-images that they held, and their violent criminal careers.

I gathered data on these four topics primarily by conducting private, informal, and in-depth interviews with offenders convicted of criminal homicide, aggravated assault, forcible and attempted forcible rape, and robbery where the victim was seriously injured. In appendix 1 I discuss how I selected the inmates for interviews, conducted my interviews with them, and validated the information that they provided me. In addition to interviewing inmates, I observed several violent actors and violent criminal acts in situ. Although completed many years before the interviews were initiated, my participant observation proved to be of invaluable assistance to me in conducting the interviews with the offenders and analyzing the data gleaned from them. I describe my participant observation in appendix 2.

Forty-seven of the fifty-eight offenders that I interviewed for this study were men, and eleven were women. Their ages ranged from midteens to late forties. A more complete description of the subjects in terms of their offenses, sex, and approximate ages is presented at the end of appendix 1.

At the time of the interviews, twenty-three of the offenders were inmates of a prison in a midwestern state,[3] and the remaining thirty-five were inmates of a jail or prisons in a far western state.

Finally, all fifty-eight offenders who served as subjects committed some type of *substantially* violent criminal act. That is, the victim was either (1) substantially physically injured, that is, nonaccidentally injured either fatally or to a degree that usually calls for a physician's attention, such as results from a shooting, stabbing, clubbing, or relentless beating; or (2) substantially sexually violated, as in the case of coitus, sodomy, fellatio, or cunnilingus, under either the threat of the infliction of substantial physical injury or the actual infliction of substantial or less severe physical injury. Thus the present study applies only to *substantially* violent criminal acts and those who commit them.

NOTES

1. See especially Mead 1964, pp. 243–47, 1936, pp. 375–85, 401–4, 1934, pp. 90–100, 117–35, 186–92; Blumer 1969, pp. 5, 12–16, 62–65, 72–73, 110–11, 1962, pp. 181–83.

2. For discussions of the generalized other, see Mead 1964, pp. 245–46, 1934, pp. 62–63, 90, 152–64, 201–2, 265, 1932, pp. 189–95; Blumer 1937, pp. 180–84; and Miller 1973, pp. 51–56.

3. In an earlier paper (1974), I presented a preliminary analysis of the data obtained from this sample. A portion of the analysis of the entire sample appeared in a later paper (1977).

4 Self as Process: Interpretation of the Situation

In the entire intellectual arsenal of the interpretive approach, there is no more potent notion than that of the "interpretation of the situation." Consequently I gathered data on the interpretations of the situations that the fifty-eight violent offenders formed when they committed their violent crimes. The information needed on these interpretive or self processes was gleaned by having these offenders describe to me in as much detail as possible what happened during the situations in which they committed their violent crimes and what, if anything, they thought and felt as these situations unfolded.

My study of these data reveals two things. First, it reveals that violent people always *do* interpret the situations in which they commit violent criminal acts. Further, the interpretations that they form of these situations account for their violent actions. In all the cases I found that the individuals committing the violent acts did at least two things. (1) By assuming the attitudes of their victims, they implicitly or explicitly indicated to themselves the meaning or character of the victim's gestures. (2) By assuming an attitude of their generalized others, they implicitly or explicitly indicated to themselves that they *ought* to take violent action. Thus the data reveal that violent people *consciously construct* violent plans of action before they commit violent criminal acts, as the examples in the following pages demonstrate.

This conclusion almost completely contradicts the previous literature on this issue. With only one exception (Hartung 1966, pp. 136–54), psychiatrists, psychologists, and sociologists have argued that most violent criminal acts are committed as a result of *unconscious* motivations, *deep* emotional needs, *inner* psychic conflicts, or sudden *unconscious* emotional bursts. For example, Banay (1952), a psychiatrist, asserts that "the true nature of the psychological phenomena of violence which causes one human being to inflict death upon another will remain shrouded in mystery unless a detailed psychiatric study traces down the inner motivations" (p. 33). Similarly Abrahamsen (1960) states that "it is safe to say that unconscious elements play an overwhelming part in homicide, and if uncovered, they will provide us with material enabling us to establish the dynamic connection between the killer's mind and his homicide" (p. 196). Tanay (1972), another psychiatrist, asserts that "ego-dystonic homicide describes a killing that occurs against the conscious wishes of the perpetrator," and he later adds that "the majority of homicides are ego-dystonic" (pp. 815, 817). Further, on the bases of their review of the literature on "murderers and murders," the Lesters (1975), two psychologists, state: "Real murderers are not usually motivated by any long-range plans or conscious desires. Most commonly, they kill during some trivial quarrel, or their acts are triggered by some apparently unimportant incident, while deep and unconscious emotional needs are their basic motivation. Most murders occur on sudden impulse and in the heat of passion, in situations where the killer's emotions overcome his ability to reason" (p. 5).

Finally, in their joint works, Wolfgang, a sociologist, and Ferracuti, a psychologist (1967a, pp. 140–41, 1967b, pp. 272–73), contend that 90 percent of criminal homicides are "passion crimes," acts that "are unplanned, explosive, determined by sudden motivational bursts" (1967a, p. 209). Wolfgang and Ferracuti (1967a) add that in such aggressive crimes the offender acts "quickly," so that "neither reasoning nor time for it are at his disposal" (p. 263).

The data from my study also reveal that the interpretations of situations in which violent criminal acts are committed are not homogeneous but fall into four distinct types. The following discussion of each of these types of interpretation should clarify how individuals construct interpretations of the situations in which they commit violent criminal acts.

PHYSICALLY DEFENSIVE INTERPRETATIONS

The first type of interpretation is "physically defensive." There are two essential steps in forming physically defensive interpretations of a situation. First, by assuming the attitude of the victim, the perpetrator implicitly or explicitly indicates to himself that the victim's gestures mean either (1) that the victim will soon physically attack him or an intimate, such as a spouse or child, or (2) that the victim is already physically attacking him or an intimate. Second, by assuming an attitude of his generalized other, the perpetrator then implicitly or explicitly indicates to himself that he ought to respond violently toward the victim and calls out within himself a violent plan of action. The perpetrator forms his violent plan of action because he sees violence as the only means of preventing another person from inflicting physical injury on him or an intimate. The key feature of all physically defensive interpretations is that the victim makes a gesture that the perpetrator designates to himself as foreshadowing or constituting a physical attack, generating a grave sense of fear in him for his own or an intimate's physical safety. Case 18 illustrates the nature of physically defensive interpretations.

Case 18: Criminal Homicide

I was sitting at a bar drinking a beer when this guy sitting next to me went to play the pinball machine. When he came back to the bar, he said, "You've been drinking my beer. I had a full can of beer when I went over to play that pinball machine." I said, "I ain't drank none of your beer." He said, "You better buy me another can of beer." I said, "Shit no, I ain't." At first I didn't know whether he really thought I had drank some of his beer or was just trying to bluff me into buying him a can, but when he later said, "You're gonna buy me another fucking can of beer," I knew then he was handing me that to start some crap, so I knew for sure that I wasn't gonna buy him any beer. He told me again to buy him a beer. I said, "Hell no." I figured if I showed him that I wasn't gonna buy him a beer, he wouldn't push it, but he said, "You better go on and buy me another fucking beer." All I said then was, "I don't want any trouble; I'm just out of the pen, so go on and leave me alone, 'cause I ain't about to buy you any beer." He just kept looking. Then I started thinking he was out to do something to me. He pulled out a knife and made for me, and I shot him once in the arm. He kept on coming, so I had to finish him off. He was out to kill me.

Further, when a perpetrator injures or kills another person as a result of forming a physically defensive interpretation, his violent criminal act is *victim precipitated*. My definition of victim precipitation is not reducible to the positivistic one that Marvin Wolfgang popularized, however. According to Wolfgang (1957), victim precipitation is where "the role of the victim is characterized by his having been the first in the homicide drama to use physical force directed against his subsequent slayer. The victim precipitated cases are those in which the victim was the first to show and use a deadly weapon, to strike a blow in an altercation—in short, the first to commence the interplay or resort to physical violence" (p. 2). In a later paper (1969) he explicitly states that the criteria that he used "to classify . . . victims as precipitators of their own deaths were based on overt physical behavior" and that "words alone were not enough" (p. 72).

Using Wolfgang's positivistic definition and my interpretive one to determine whether to classify violent criminal acts as victim precipitated readily shows the differences between our respective definitions. First, a violent criminal act can be victim precipitated according to Wolfgang's definition and also follow from a physically defensive interpretation. The individual takes violent action in such a case, but only after indicating to himself that his antagonists have already physically attacked him or an intimate and through further self-indication judges that physical retaliation is the best means of preventing his antagonists from inflicting further injuries on him or an intimate. Second, a violent criminal act can be non–victim precipitated according to Wolfgang's definition but follow from a physically defensive interpretation. Here the individual resorts to physical violence first but does so only after indicating to himself that his antagonists' gestures indicate that a physical attack on him or an intimate is imminent and through further self-indication judges that a preemptive strike is the best means of protecting his or an intimate's physical safety. Third, a violent criminal act can be non–victim precipitated according to Wolfgang's definition and also not follow from a physically defensive interpretation. In this case the perpetrator resorts to physical violence first, but without forming a physically defensive interpretation of the situation. Before taking his violent action, the individual neither indicates to himself that his protagonists are either physically attacking him or an intimate or threatening to do so nor through further self-indication judges that a retaliatory or preemptive strike is the best means of stopping their present or soon anticipated physical attack on him or an intimate.

Finally, a violent criminal act can be victim precipitated according to Wolfgang's definition but not follow from a physically defensive interpretation. Here the victim strikes first, but the blow struck is so slight that the perpetrator does not define it as imperiling either him or an intimate, as in the case of a bumping. If physical gestures that are not physically threatening are considered to satisfy the requirement for victim precipitation, however, then it becomes necessary for the sake of consistency to consider as well physical gestures where no physical contact is made with the perpetrator, as in the case of obscene gestures. Consequently, if the victim made any physical gesture toward the perpetrator before being attacked, then the violent criminal act would have to be considered as victim precipitated.

The relationship between these two ways of defining victim precipitation not only makes it clear that the two definitions are not synonymous. It also exposes the fundamental weakness in Wolfgang's positivistic definition of victim precipitation. The positivistic conception ignores the meaning of precipitation to the victim and offender. Moreover Wolfgang's deprecation of the importance of "words" in precipitating physical altercations is at odds not only with the interpretive approach taken here but also now with criminal law (*People vs. Berry* 1976; *People vs. Valentine* 1946). Thus the positivistic conception leaves out far too many cases in which the victim *is* a genuine contributing factor in the offense and includes far too many cases in which the victim is *not* a genuinely contributing factor in the offense.

FRUSTRATIVE INTERPRETATIONS

The second type of interpretation of situations in which violent criminal acts are committed is "frustrative." Frustrative interpretations are formed in two basic steps. First, by assuming the attitude of the victim, the perpetrator implicitly or explicitly indicates to himself that the victim's gestures mean either (1) that the victim is resisting or will resist the *specific* course of action that the perpetrator seeks to carry out or (2) that the perpetrator should cooperate in a *specific* course of action that he does not want carried out. Second, by assuming an attitude of his generalized other, the perpetrator then implicitly or explicitly indicates to himself that he ought to respond violently toward the victim and calls out within himself a violent plan of action. The perpetrator forms this violent plan of action because he sees violence as the most appropriate way to handle another person's potential or attempted blockage of the larger act that the perpetrator wants to carry out—for example, robbery, sexual intercourse, car theft—or to block the larger act that the other person wants to carry out—for example, calling the police or arresting the perpetrator. The mark of all frustrative interpretations is that the perpetrator becomes angry after designating to himself the direction along which the larger act is heading and his desire for the act not to follow that course. Cases 49 and 10 illustrate the two ways that individuals form frustrative interpretations.

Case 49: Forcible Rape

I was listening to the radio in my apartment when I got horny and started thinking about getting me some pussy. I thought that I'd go down to the ——— district and find a nice white broad to bust my nut in. I knew the area pretty good, and it was far enough away from my own house. So I went out and jumped the ——— bus. I rode it to ——— Street and then got off and started walking around. I got a good look at this middle-aged white broad walking around some apartments, and I said to myself, "I'm going to get that pussy and enjoy it."

I followed her up to the entrance of an apartment building. She used a key to get into the main door, and I had to get to it fast before it shut. I barely got to the door in time, but I waited a few seconds before I walked in, since I didn't want her to see me. When I went in, I heard her going up the stairs, and I followed her. As soon as I got to the top of the stairs, I spotted her walking down the hallway, and I crept up behind her. When she opened the door to her apartment, I put my hands over her mouth, pushed her through the door, and said, "Don't make a sound." Then I shut the door behind me and said, "If you make one fucking sound, I'll kill your ass."

I didn't want her to panic too soon, so I threw her off base and said, "Do you have any money?" She said, "All I have is the $10 in my church envelope." I said, "Well, give it here." She took the envelope out of her purse and handed it to me. Then I said, "Take your coat off." I took a long look at her and thought, "I'm going to drive this broad all night long."

I grabbed her by the shoulders and threw her to the floor. She started yelling, "What are you doing? What are you doing?" I figured that I better let her know that I meant business, so I jumped right on her ass and started smashing her in the face and saying, "Shut up, shut up." As soon as she did, I stopped hitting her. Then I pulled her dress up above her waist and reached for her meat, and she started screaming "Stop, stop, stop" and stomped the floor with her feet. I just thought, "I have got to shut her ass up fast before somebody hears her," and then I really cut loose on her with lefts and rights and said, "Shut up, shut up, before I beat you to death." Finally she shut the fuck up, and I pulled her dress back up, tore her panties off her legs, and pulled out my rod. I got on her and put my rod up to her meat. When she felt it going in her, she yelled, "No, no, stop, stop," but I kept driving it on in her. I wanted to drive her all night, but I came. Although I came faster than I wanted, I busted my nut good. After I zipped up my pants, I said, "Don't move," and split out the door.[1]

Case 10: Criminal Homicide

I was low on cash and had heard about a good place to make a hit. About an hour later my friend and I were punching the safe when a real young cop came in with his gun drawn and said, "You're under arrest; put your hands up." The first thing I thought was, "Here is ten years, and I don't want to do any more fucking time." I decided then that I wasn't going to give myself up. The cop walked up closer to us, and I thought about getting his gun away from him, but I wondered where his partner was. He looked nervous, scared. I thought in the back of my mind that he would not use the gun, but I didn't care either. Then I figured he didn't have any partner and about hitting him. I had to get out of the situation. When he got right up to us, I hit him with the hammer.

MALEFIC INTERPRETATIONS

The third type of interpretation of situations in which violent criminal acts are committed is "malefic." Malefic interpretations are formed in a three-step process. First, by assuming the attitude of the victim, the perpetrator implicitly or explicitly indicates to himself that the victim's gestures mean that the victim is deriding or badly belittling the perpetrator. Second, by assuming an attitude of his generalized other, the perpetrator implicitly or explicitly indicates to himself that the victim is an extremely evil or malicious person. Finally, by making further self-indications from the same attitude of his generalized other, the perpetrator implicitly or explicitly indicates to himself that he ought to respond violently toward the victim and calls out within himself a violent plan of action. The perpetrator forms his violent plan of action because he sees violence as the most fitting way of handling evil or malicious people who make derogatory gestures. The key feature of all malefic interpretations is that the perpetrator judges the victim to be extremely evil or malicious, which in turn ignites his hatred for the victim. Case 35 illustrates how an individual forms a malefic interpretation.

Case 35: Aggravated Assault

I was just cruising around with some friends of mine, drinking wine, smoking dope, and eating a few reds. We came to an intersection and slowed down to make a turn when this black dude in a Thunderbird coming the other way cut us off in the middle of the intersection while he made a turn. Then he drove by us with a big grin on his face throwing the bone. The friend of mine who was driving just turned and started going the other way, but I suddenly said to myself, "That dirty jive nigger flipping me off and grinning—now he thinks he's one bad nigger. Well, I'm going to get down with that black motherfucker." Then I grabbed the wheel and said, "Turn around and catch that nigger driving that Thunderbird." We started following him, but after he made a couple of turns, we lost him. He was too far ahead of us. I said, "Well, he's got to be somewhere in this neighborhood, so let's just keep driving around here until we spot that Thunderbird, because I'm out to book that nigger." I could still see his big grin when he shot us the bird, and it was driving me up a wall. There was just no way that I was going to quit looking for that motherfucker. I was outright determined to have his ass one way or another.

Finally I spotted his car in a driveway in front of a house, and I told X, who was driving, to pull over and park in front of the house. Then I snapped my shotgun together and loaded it. One of my friends said, "Hey, Y, what the hell is your trip?" I said, "It's just my trip," and jumped out of the car. I didn't care about anything but having that nigger's ass. All I thought was, "I'm going to kill this punk." I walked up to the house and knocked on the front door. He answered the door, but as soon as he saw it was me, he slammed it shut in my face. Then I kicked the door wide open and saw him making tracks out the back door. I ran through the house after him and jammed him as he was climbing over the back fence. I leveled the barrel of my shotgun at his head and said, "Nigger, get off that fence." After he did, I said, "Head back into that house." I wanted to fuck him up in the house so nobody would see it, but when we got to the back door, he stopped and said, "Man, I haven't done anything to you. Please don't hurt me." His sniveling made me madder. I shoved the barrel into his back and said, "Man, go into that house." He still wouldn't go in but just kept begging me not to shoot him. This pissed me off even more. I lost all my patience and said, "Fuck it," and shot him right where he was standing.

FRUSTRATIVE-MALEFIC INTERPRETATIONS

The final type of interpretation of situations in which violent criminal acts are committed is "frustrative-malefic," which combines features of the prior two types. Frustrative-malefic interpretations are formed in a three-step process. First, by assuming the attitude of the victim, the perpetrator implicitly or explicitly indicates to himself that the victim's gestures mean either that the victim is resisting some *specific* line of action that the perpetrator wants to carry out or that he wants the perpetrator to cooperate in some *specific* line of action that the perpetrator does not want carried out. Second, by assuming an attitude of his generalized other, the perpetrator implicitly or explicitly indicates to himself that the victim's gestures are irksome or malicious and consequently that the victim is evil or malicious. Finally, by making further self-indications from the same attitude of his generalized other, the perpetrator implicitly or explicitly indicates to himself that he ought to respond violently toward the victim and calls out within himself a violent plan of action. The perpetrator forms this violent plan of action because he sees violence as the most appropriate way to deal with an evil or malicious person's potential or attempted blockage of the larger act that he seeks to carry out or as the most appropriate way to block the larger act that an evil or malicious person wants to carry out. The perpetrator views the victim not only as an adversary but as a particularly loathsome one as well (see Shibutani 1970). The mark of all frustrative-malefic interpretations is that they start out as frustrative interpretations. Before the perpetrator mounts his violent attack, however, the interpretations become malefic, with pure hatred always displacing the anger that the perpetrator earlier felt toward his victim. Case 21 illustrates the nature of frustrative-malefic interpretations.

Case 21: Aggravated Assault

I was at a neighborhood tavern drinking beer next to this guy who I knew was a homosexual. He was showing his billfold around, and I began to think about hustling him. We were in the bathroom together several times and I tried to hustle him, but he acted sneaky [he didn't put up any money], so I punched him. He then left the tavern threatening to call the police on me. I thought, "That motherfucking queer, I should rob him and bust his fucking head." So I followed him. He went home. I knocked on his door, but he wouldn't answer. I got mad and kicked his door open. Then this guy, his boyfriend, who was shacking up with him, comes up to me. His boyfriend being there got me madder, so I punched the boyfriend. The boyfriend took off out the front door. I then caught that queer standing there watching and staring at me. This got me madder. I figured this was a good opportunity to rob him and mess him up too. I've gone this far, so I might as well go all the way and do a good job on him. I'm in trouble as it is. You can get just as much time for doing a good job as a bad one. I wanted to fuck him up. I started beating him.

NOTE

1. In the original edition I stopped the presentation of case 49 at the point where the subject reported, "I pulled her dress back up, tore her panties off her legs and. . . ." I did not include this entire case in the original edition out of fear that it might offend some readers' moral sensibilities. Since that time I have changed my position on this matter. I now believe that readers need to be confronted with the full, ugly reality of violent crime not only to enlarge their understanding of these offenses but to prevent them from romanticizing their perpetrators.

5 When Interpretations of Situations Lead

to Violent Criminal Acts

The data on the interpretations of situations described in chapter 4 pertain only to situations in which the individuals committed a violent criminal act; that is, they were *completed* violent situations. In other words, I collected these data in a retrospective fashion, starting from the fact that a violent criminal act was committed rather than from the interpretive process that preceded the act. Thus I could conclude from these data only that whenever an actor committed a substantially violent criminal act, he necessarily formed a physically defensive, frustrative, malefic, or frustrative-malefic interpretation. This leaves open the question of whether a violent criminal act is committed every time an individual forms one of these four interpretations.

This question can be addressed by gathering data on interpretations that violent offenders made of situations in which they almost committed a violent criminal act but did not do so, that is, of near-violent situations. I did this by having the offenders describe to me in the most detailed fashion possible what, if anything, they indicated to themselves and how, if at all, they judged these self-indications during situations in which they almost committed violent criminal acts. Since my study of these materials reveals that the interpretations of near-violent situations fall into the same four types already described for completed violent situations, I compared the interpretations of completed violent and near-violent situations of the same type. More specifically, I compared the physically defensive, frustrative, malefic, and frustrative-malefic interpretations that were formed in completed violent situations with those formed in near-violent situations.

My comparisons of interpretations formed in completed violent situations and those formed in near-violent ones reveal that the occurrence or nonoccurrence of three possible events determined whether a violent criminal act was committed. The first event I term a "fixed line of indication."

FIXED LINE OF INDICATION

A fixed line of indication occurs when an individual continues to call out within himself a violent plan of action until he physically attacks his antagonists. After forming a violent interpretation, he fails to consider anything else in the situation besides acting violently. He either immediately carries out his violent plan of action or further nurtures it along by continuing to indicate to himself from the same attitude of his generalized other that he ought to respond violently, until he finally does carry out the plan of action. He thus falls prey to "tunnel vision." Case 33 illustrates an individual who formed a malefic interpretation and then stayed in a fixed line of indication.

Case 33: Aggravated Assault

I was over at my partner's pad drinking wine and smoking dope late one night, and I called a taxi to take me home since I had wrecked my car. The driver pulled up, and I ran out. I opened the door to his taxi, and he asked me where I was going. I told him to ———— Street in ————, and he said, "Well, that's over a ten-mile trip. You'll have to pay me the fare in advance before I'll drive you there." I got mad as shit because I wanted to get home, and I didn't have any cash to be paying him in advance with. I said, "You're fucking crazy, old man. I've taken a taxi there many times at night and never had to pay in advance. My dad will pay you your money as soon as we get there. Here's my wallet; you can look at my name." He said, "All right, get in. Don't get shook up—I believe you. I don't need to see your wallet."

As soon as we took off, he started telling me about all the times that he had been burned by people taking his cab. I just said to myself, "Why is this old bastard telling me all this shit? I'm not going to rip him off. I told him that I was going to pay him." I just sat in the back of the taxi not saying a word, and he kept on telling me about how people were always ripping him off, along with all the other problems that he had. I thought, "Man, I've got five times as many troubles as he has. He must really be a weak person to be telling someone that he doesn't even know all about his personal problems. I don't want to hear this bullshit." Finally his crying to me set my blood boiling. The old fucker was really irking me.

When he drove the taxi down the street that my house was on, I said to myself, "This old motherfucker handed me all that shit before I could even get in his taxi, and he has been sniveling to me the whole fucking time I've been riding in it. Fucking SOB, I'm going to cut his stinking throat." As soon as he stopped the cab, I opened up my knife and put the blade to him.

Case 37 illustrates an individual who formed a physically defensive interpretation and then stayed in a fixed line of indication.

Case 37: Criminal Homicide

I was over at my friend's place, just sitting around drinking whiskey with him and another guy. This other dude then came over, and we began shooting dice for half-dollars. After about an hour or so of shooting dice, I started feeling the whiskey and decided that I better be leaving. I told them that I had to go, and I picked up my dice and put them in my pocket. Then X jumped up and said, "What did you pick up those dice for?" I said, "Because I'm finished shooting, and I'm going to split." He said, "You can't quit now. You have to give me a chance to win back some of my money." I couldn't understand him coming down on me with that because I hadn't won that much money. I said, "Hey, man, I'm tired of shooting, and I've got to be somewhere now."

Then he got right up in my face and said, "You're not quitting yet, motherfucker." I thought to myself, "There's no use trying to talk to him; reasoning with him is out of the question," so I said, "The hell if I'm not. I told you that I'm tired of playing." He stared at me with his eyes popping out of his head like he was crazy and said, "You dirty, no-good fucking-ass punk." I figured then that I was in a hell of a situation. I knew that the drunken fool wasn't in his right state of mind, and I got scared because I knew he carried a gun and didn't care what he did. I heard that he had killed a dude some time back.

I said, "Man, will you get the fuck out of my face?" But that sent him into a rage. He started swinging his arms side to side and calling me a motherfucking punk, and he spit in my face. I called him a dirty motherfucker, and he shoved me. I figured then that he wasn't going to be wasting much more time on me, and when he went into his coat, I thought that he was reaching for his piece. I knew then that I had to act quick, so I pulled out my pistol and shot the crazy damn fool before he could shoot me. I knew that he'd shoot me without any hesitation. I was just damn lucky that I had bought a gun after being mugged about a week before.[1]

RESTRAINING JUDGMENT

The second event that may occur is a "restraining judgment." This happens when the individual breaks out of his fixed line of indication and decides that he should not carry out his violent plan of action. Here the individual escapes from his tunnel vision. He *redefines* the situation and on the basis of his new definition judges that he should not act violently. In forming a restraining judgment, the individual completely drops or shelves the violent plan of action that he had built up, and his violent interpretation of the situation subsides. The occurrence of restraining judgments dispels the old, but still surprisingly prevalent, belief that violent crimes are "acts of passion" devoid of all reason. The study of these near-violent situations reveals several types of reasons individuals form restraining judgments.[2]

First, an individual may form a restraining judgment in a situation because he fears that he will fail. By assuming the attitude of the person whom he had planned to attack, the individual implicitly or explicitly indicates to himself that the intended victim will retaliate if physically attacked. Then, by assuming an attitude of his generalized other, the individual implicitly or explicitly indicates to himself that he should not carry out his violent plan of action because he would be unsuccessful in a physical altercation with the other person. Case 34 is an example of an individual who formed a malefic interpretation and then restrained it for this reason.

Case 34: Near-Violent Situation

I was in jail. I saw a newspaper laying open on a table, so I sat down and started reading it. Then this dude came up out of nowhere and said, "Don't be fucking with anything on my end of that table." I said, "I don't see any name on this table or that paper." He said, "Everything on this end of the table is mine, and I don't fuck around with niggers or white folks." I thought to myself, "What a sick, stupid motherfucker." As I got up and walked away from the table, I said to this other dude, "What the fuck is wrong with that crazy SOB?" When he heard me say that, he charged up to me and said, "Motherfucker, you don't have to ask anybody about me." I really didn't want any fight with the dude because he looked pretty bad; he had big old arms and shoulders, and some of his teeth were missing. So I only said, "Man, you must be crazy. What is wrong with your ass?" Then he fired on me. He hit me hard and downed me. Then I saw that he had opened up my fucking nose. I really got hot. I just thought I wanted to kill that dirty SOB. I jumped up to my feet and pulled out a finger-nail file that I had on me. But then I thought, "This file won't stop him, and he's too fucking big to fight without something more than this. I better back off." After I backed up a few feet, I said, "Mother-fucker, don't you ever turn your back near me. You've busted my fucking nose, and I'm going to get you for it." He looked at me and said, "Come on, do it right now." I just said, "I'll catch you later," and walked off fast, real fast.

Second, an individual may form a restraining judgment in a situation because the other person has suddenly changed his course of action. By assuming the attitude of the person whom he had planned to attack, the individual implicitly or explicitly indicates to himself that the physically threatening, malicious, or frustrating gestures have been altered or halted. Next, by assuming an attitude of his generalized other, the individual implicitly or explicitly indicates to himself that he no longer needs to carry out his violent plan of action. Case 55 illustrates an individual who formed a frustrative interpretation and then restrained it for this reason.

Case 55: Near-Violent Situation

I needed to score, but my money wasn't right, so I started thinking about where I could get the coin. I decided that I was going to have to go out and rob some fucking place. Then I started thinking about different places to hit. My mind first turned to this Dairy Queen, but I figured that it wouldn't be worth the trouble since there wouldn't be much money there anyway. Then I started thinking about this small supermarket, but I dropped that idea for the same reason. Finally a cleaner's flashed in my mind. I figured that it would be the best hit since there would be enough money and only old ladies worked there. I put on my sunglasses, grabbed my .45, took off the safety clip, and headed for the cleaner's. I walked in the place, pulled out my pistol, and pointed it at the old lady behind the counter. I said, "This is a holdup. I don't want to shoot you, so give me all the money out of that cash register fast." She walked over to the cash register but then just stopped and said, "I'm not going to give you this money," and stepped on a button on the floor.

I told myself I was going to get that money. I leaned over the counter and put the barrel of my pistol in her face and said, "Lady, now I'm going to kill you." But just as I was going to pull the trigger, she opened the cash register drawer and said, "You can get the money yourself." I then told her to get away from the cash register, and she did. After I grabbed all the paper money, she smiled and said, "I guess I don't know much about you youngsters these days." I looked at her for a moment and thought that she was just a nice, old, batty grandmother. Then I split fast.

Third, an individual may form a restraining judgment because he fears that he will seriously damage or possibly destroy the social relationship, such as friendship or marriage, that exists between him and the other person. By assuming the attitude of the person whom he had planned to attack, the individual implicitly or explicitly indicates to himself that this person might end or drastically change their relationship if assaulted. Next, by assuming an attitude of his generalized other, he implicitly or explicitly indicates to himself that he should not carry out his violent plan of action because he does not want to jeopardize his social relationship with this person. Case 58 illustrates how an individual who formed a frustrative-malefic interpretation restrained it for this reason.

Case 58: Near-Violent Situation

I was at home looking for the TV guide when I found a note written by my wife. It said that she owed somebody $6 for babysitting for her twelve hours. I thought to myself, "Where in the living hell could she have been gone for twelve hours?" My mind then turned to her stepping out with someone behind my back, so I called her. When she came in the room, I said, "What in the hell is this note about?" She grabbed the note out of my hand and said, "Oh, it's nothing." I said, "What in the hell do you mean that it's nothing? Where in the hell were you for twelve hours?"

Then she started giving me some story about going shopping and to the hairdresser's. I said, "Bullshit, that crap doesn't take any twelve hours to do." She said, "Well, maybe the twelve hours that I wrote on the note is a mistake." I said, "Don't hand me that bullshit. You're fucking around with someone." She said, "No, no, I'm not." Then I yelled, "You no-good tramp, dirty whore, you better tell me where in the hell you have been." She said, "You are acting like nothing but a bum. I'm not going to tell you anything." I thought to myself, "I'm going to beat the damn truth out of that no-good, rotten bitch." I started thinking about tying her up and beating her until she talked, but then I thought that if I went that far, she might leave me, so I dropped it. I was scared that if I did do it, then I would end up losing her.

Fourth, an individual may form a restraining judgment out of deference to another person. By assuming the attitude of a person whose opinion is important to him, the individual implicitly or explicitly indicates to himself that this person does not desire him to act violently. Next, by assuming an attitude of his generalized other, the actor implicitly or explicitly indicates to himself that he should not carry out his violent plan of action because he wants to respect this person's wishes. Case 32 is an example of an individual who formed a malefic interpretation and then restrained it for this reason.

Case 32: Near-Violent Situation

I was at a bar where I used to spend a lot of time when the bartender told me that X had come in earlier looking for me. I didn't think too much about it at the time, but a little while later she came back. As soon as she saw me, she charged up to me and said, "Bitch, I've been looking for you. What in the hell did you think you were doing running out on me the other night?" I looked at her and thought to myself, "This bulldagging bitch must think she owns me. I don't have to own up to her or anybody else." Then she said, "Well, bitch, what have you got to say for yourself?" I had had enough of her phony ass then, and I said, "Bitch, you better get out of my face. You don't control what I do. I do what I please." She said, "Bitch, you better watch how you talk to me, 'cause I'll get into your ass." My mind turned to cutting her then and doing it fast. I grabbed my razor and said, "Bitch, I'm going to cut you up so bad that they won't be able to sew your ass up." But before I could get to her with it, Y jumped in between us and said, "Be cool; don't be doing anything like that." I really wanted to hurt that bitch, but out of due respect to Y, I dropped it. If he hadn't asked me to leave her alone, I would have cut her ass up so bad it wouldn't have been funny.

Fifth, an individual may form a restraining judgment because he fears possible legal sanction. By assuming the attitude of other people who are physically present, he indicates to himself that they will witness his assault on the intended victim. Next, by assuming an attitude of his generalized other, he implicitly or explicitly indicates to himself that he should not carry out his violent plan of action at this time if he does not want to be arrested or incarcerated for the attack. The individual's perceived longer-term interest may permanently halt or merely temporarily delay his execution of the particular violent plan of action. Case 54 illustrates an individual who formed a frustrative interpretation and then restrained it for this reason.

Case 54: Near-Violent Situation

I was doing some Christmas shopping at a shopping center in my neighborhood. I was going through the stores looking for things to get for my family when I started picking up on the women shopping near me. Then I just stopped in the middle of the shopping plaza and looked at the women who walked by. While I was standing there checking them out good, my dick got on a big hard. I was tripping on butt fucking some of the broads who walked by with real nice plump asses and slim waists when the idea came to me to rip one of them off. I decided to do it, so I went and stole a carving knife from a grocery store and then walked out to the corner of the parking lot of the shopping center. I wanted to find a broad with a nice full ass walking alone to her car. I figured that I'd jump into her car with her and then make her drive out to a deserted area nearby that I knew about. I was watching people going to their cars when I spotted this broad with a nice face and big hips and a fat, round ass walking by herself. She looked like an easy rip-off, so I started following her and snuck up right behind her. When she stuck her keys in her car door, I grabbed her by the arm, flashed my knife in her face, and said, "Get into your car and don't make any noise." She just stood there like she was in a complete daze.

So I let go of her arm and grabbed her car keys and opened the car door myself. I told her to get in because we were going for a ride, but she just started screaming her ass off. First I decided to force her into the car, and I grabbed onto her again, but she kept on screaming and started getting away from me. I figured that other people were probably seeing by now what was happening, so I thought I had better get the hell out of there fast before I got busted. Then I booked it, and she ran off toward the stores screaming.

OVERRIDING JUDGMENT

The final event that determines whether an interpretation of a situation will lead to a violent act is an "overriding judgment." This happens when the individual breaks out of a fixed line of indication and escapes from his tunnel vision only to reenter it later. Here he either momentarily considers restraining his violent plan of action or actually forms a restraining judgment but then redefines the situation and rejudges it as definitely calling for violent action. After forming a violent interpretation of the situation, the individual restrains his violent plan of action; he then again redefines the situation and judges that he should now go ahead and carry out the plan of action. My study of completed violent situations reveals that the primary reason individuals form overriding judgments is because they judge the victim's conduct to be intolerable. By assuming the attitude of the victim, the individual implicitly or explicitly indicates to himself that the victim is continuing his physically threatening, frustrating, or malicious course of action. Then, by assuming an attitude of his generalized other, the individual implicitly or explicitly indicates to himself that he should go ahead and carry out his violent plan of action at all costs because the intended victim's gestures have now become unendurable. Case 32 illustrates how an individual overruled a restraining judgment for this reason after she had formed a malefic interpretation.[3]

Case 32: Aggravated Assault

We were partying one night in my rooms at the hotel where I lived and worked. Everybody there was a regular, except for this one dude who I had rented a room down the hall. He just kind of drifted in, and X said that he knew the dude, so it was cool. We were all drinking wine, taking pills, and having a mellow time when I overheard this dude asking X who I was and saying that I was a bitch. I said,

"Hey, who's the bitch you are talking about?" and he said, "You're the bitch." I thought to myself, "What does this dude think he's doing, coming to my party uninvited and then calling me a fucking bitch?" I said, "Don't you come to my party and call me a bitch." He said, "You are a bitch; I was high and you shortchanged me out of fucking $20 when I paid you for my room today." I said, "Man, you are crazy." He said, "Don't try to slick me, bitch; I'm hip. I'm an ex-con. I know what's happening, and X knows I'm good people, so don't try to run that game on me."

My friends were having a good time, I felt good, and I didn't want to spoil the mood for any problems behind $20, so I thought that I'd just pacify the chump and give him a lousy $20 and end it. I said, "Look, man, I didn't shortchange you out of any money today, but just to show my good heart, I'll give you $20. How about that?" He said, "Well, since you needed it so fucking bad that you had to try to run a game like that past me, then you can keep it, bitch." Then I thought that motherfucker was just messing with me. He was trying to make me out as a petty hustler and call me a bitch right in front of my friends. I said to myself, "Please, motherfucker, don't mess with me any more." I finally said, "Mister, I'm warning you, don't you fuck with me any more or I'll show you what a fucking bitch is." He just looked at me, laughed, and said, "I haven't seen the bitch yet who could kick my ass."

Then I told myself, "This man has got to go, one way or another. I've just had enough of this motherfucker messing with me. I'm going to cut his dirty, motherfucking throat." I went into my bedroom, got a $20 bill and my razor. I said to myself, "The motherfucker wouldn't stop fucking with me, and now he's hung himself," and I walked out of the bedroom. I went up to him with a big smile on my face. I held the $20 bill in my hand out in front of me and hid the razor in my other hand. Then I sat on his lap and said, "Okay, you're a fast dude. Here's your $20 back." He said, "I'm glad that you are finally admitting it." I looked at him with a smile and said, "Let me seal it with a kiss." I said to myself, "Motherfucker, now I'll show you what a fucking bitch is," and then I bent over like I was going to kiss him and started slicing up his throat.

Case 24 is another example of an individual who overruled a restraining judgment for this same reason after he had formed a frustrative-malefic interpretation.

Case 24: Aggravated Assault

My brother and I met this dude at a bar where we were drinking and cutting it up. The dude invited us over to his place to drink some beer after the bar closed. We wanted to crash there for the night. We got a couple of six-packs and took a cab over to his pad. Then, after we finished drinking all of the beer, the dude dropped the bombshell and said, "Look, you guys are going to have to leave now." I said, "Hell, why didn't you tell us that before we came over here?" He said, "Well, I'm telling you that now." I thought to myself, "We bought the beer, paid for the cab, and haven't gotten out of line; this dude is just using us," so I said, "I'm not going anywhere. There are no buses or cabs running now. I'm not going out on that street hitchhiking this time of night." I was ready to fuck his loud, smart ass up, but my brother said, "Come on, X, let's go." I decided that he was right and I would go on and listen to him and split rather than start a hassle. But then the dude pushed me and said, "You heard what I said, now go on and get the fuck out of here." I said, "Look, don't you push me," but then he pushed me again. I thought, "This smart-ass nickel-and-dime drunk thinks he can just shit all over us," and I told him, "I'm leaving, so don't you push me again or I'll fuck you up." Then my brother said, "Come on, let's just go. Fuck this dude." The dude said, "That's right, get your fucking ass out of here now," and pushed me once more. I said to myself, "Fuck it, that's it, I'm going to fuck him up." I hit him with a right hook, went berserk, and grabbed a lamp and busted him over the head and downed him. I yelled, "You punk motherfucker, I'll kick your eyes out of your head," and stomped him in the face, knocking his teeth out of his mouth and swelling shut both his eyes. Then I kept kicking him and kicking him hard as I could in the ribs until my brother finally grabbed me and said, "Come on, we gotta split out here now."[4]

In short, in the completed violent situations that I studied, the subjects always either entered into a fixed line of indication or else formed an overriding judgment, whereas in the near-violent situations that I studied, the subjects always formed a restraining judgment. Once people have formed violent plans of action, whether they carry them out depends on what happens during the process of interpretation, that is, on whether they stay in a fixed line of indication or form a restraining or overriding judgment. Unsurprisingly, people form restraining judgments far more often than they form overriding ones or become locked in fixed lines of indication. Consequently—and fortunately—far more violent criminal acts are begun than are ever completed.

NOTES

1. For other examples of perpetrators who stayed in a fixed line of indication after forming other types of violent interpretations, see the cases presented in chapter 4.

2. I should mention that individuals may form restraining judgments for types of reasons other than those presented here.

3. For additional examples of perpetrators who overruled the restraining judgment that they made after forming a violent interpretation, see cases 57 and 29 in chapter 7.

4. In the original edition I stopped the presentation of case 24 at "'You punk motherfucker, I'll kick your eyes out of your head' and stomped him in the face. . . ." In note 1 to chapter 4 I explain my reasons for excluding this material from the original and for including it in this edition.

6 Self as Object: Self-Images

From the interpretive point of view, one of the most vital facts that can be known about human beings is how they see themselves, their self-portraits. Of course, sufficient attention must be always paid to the date when the self-portrait was painted. Consequently I gathered data on the self-images that the fifty-eight offenders held *at the time of their violent offenses.* I gleaned this highly pertinent information by having the offenders describe themselves to me during this period of their lives. More specifically, I asked them (1) how they thought of themselves during that time, (2) how they thought others—that is, intimates such as best friends, spouses, or siblings—thought of them during that time, and (3) whether these others saw them correctly and why. My study of these data reveals that the self-images of individuals who have committed substantial violent criminal acts fall into three types: *violent, incipiently violent,* and *nonviolent.*[1]

VIOLENT SELF-IMAGES

Violent self-images have two hallmarks. First, the actors are seen by others and see themselves as having a *violent disposition,* that is, a willingness or readiness to attack other people physically with the intention of seriously harming them. Second, the actors are seen by others and see themselves as having violence-related personal attributes (such as being mean, ill-tempered, hotheaded, coldhearted, explosive, or forceful) as a *salient* characteristic. Case 35 illustrates a man in his early twenties who was convicted of aggravated assault and who held a violent self-image at the time of his offense.

Case 35: Aggravated Assault

I was a low rider. I loved to get loaded and drive fast or just kick back and listen to hard rock, drink wine, smoke dope, and wrench my high-powered motor. I liked anything mechanical that went fast. I was free-wheeling; one day I'd be in Frisco, the next in San Diego, putting, wired up, all night long. I did plenty of good fucking too. My old lady worked, so I could just lay back and watch the river go by. Every now and then, though, I'd have to supplement what she brought home with some heavy hustling of my own, like armed robberies and other things. My old lady and ace partner both thought I was a good heavy-hustling motherfucker.

When I got bored with all that then, I might go out scrapping. I was a quiet dude but enjoyed touching up a dude that was loud. If I heard a dude talking loud about a lot of shit, it upset me inside. Once that happened, I wanted to get it on, check out the dude's oil and find out if he was a quart low. I was not often ever scared of anybody or anything. I'd seen life come and go.

My number-one old lady thought more or less the same about me. She thought if I could just cage my temper that I wouldn't be a half-bad guy. She knew when I was hot, I was a mad animal, and even when I was cool, I still acted like a barbarian. I was just the loosest motherfucker that she ever met; she thought I just didn't give a fuck about a thing. I spent money too freely, used too many drugs, and nutted up too much. People used to wonder how come a fine, foxy woman like her put up with a dude like me, but she did. I was her main squeeze, and she never went south on me.

My ace tramp partner thought of me as a pretty jam-up dude. He knew that I'd always back his play and that there would never be any slack on my part. He thought that I was just a low rider at heart who just liked to get loaded, ride fast, and fight. He thought that I was down with it when it came to hopping up motors and that I didn't fuck with any dogs. He also knew the three things that I gave a fuck about and didn't let anybody mess with—my old lady, my kid, and my motorcycle.

Nothing else really mattered to me. The philosophy that I followed was that you do whatever you want to do, when and how you want to do it, and fuck everything and everybody else. This meant to me that you had the most balls, you did the most outrageous things; in other words, that you were one of the most terrible motherfuckers who ever walked the streets. I was caught up in trying to live up to this twenty-four hours a day. That was me.

Participant-observation case 1 illustrates a man in his late forties who held a violent self-image. I observed some of the substantial violent acts that he committed in which the police did and did not intervene. This case is particularly important because it illustrates the violent self-image of an individual who had not undergone any prison socialization.

Participant-Observation Case 1

I'm X the [nationality]. I'm a man, not a boy, and I don't need any titty bottle to suck on. I want to be treated like a man too. I don't go bumming around people's houses and asking them, "What you got to eat?" I don't eat over at other people's houses, period. People know that I got groceries in my icebox. I don't have my old lady working either. I buy all the groceries and pay the bills in my house, so what I say goes. It better damn sight go. I'm the king of my house, and if somebody doesn't like it, then they can just get the fuck out. There are no locks on my doors. I don't care how other people run their houses. If someone is living under my roof and eating my food, then they better do what I say whether they like it or not. And they all know it too.

I'm a hardworking SOB, and I deserve some respect for it. I work a regular job, but I make my livelihood by working on the side too. I'm a natural hustler. I know how to talk to people. I was born with the gift of gab. I can sell anybody. I can go out there anytime and make myself some extra money. I don't need any college degrees or union cards to do it either. I don't need to wait for payday every week to get my money. I can make it on any day of the week. I don't give a damn how many union cards or degrees a person has; I can outmake them three to one. Shit, I can go out there and make in one day what those poor bastards slave to make all week, and if I have a good day, I can make more money than they'll make in a month. I don't have to ask people to lend me a couple of bucks till payday. I don't have to go around saying that I have this or that degree or union card; I just flash the roll in my wallet. Talk is cheap. Money is what talks in this world, and my mind is always on how to make a buck.

I just don't have time for hobbies and mess like most people do. I got too many mouths to feed. Everybody in my house is depending on me and on what I bring home, so I don't waste my time collecting things, talking about politics, and reading the paper or books trying to impress people with how much I know. That horseshit won't buy you anything. While those people are sitting on their fat asses talking about this or that or messing around with their hobbies, I'm out there making a buck. I'm no fool or dummy.

Of course, this doesn't mean that I don't ever like to have fun. I'll lay a bet or two on the World Series, Superbowl, and things like that. I also enjoy taking a sociable drink every day, but I'm not a drunk. I don't stay out of work drunk, and you won't find me staggering around my house or falling out in the damn street. I'm no wino, and I have never been one. I'm not what you would call a sick alcoholic, like some people I know.

I'm a man, and I want to be treated like a man. Hell, I'm real easy to get along with just as long as people don't take me too light. I just don't play. When I tell somebody something, I mean it. I don't want to hear a whole lot of horseshit about who did what. I don't care who a person is or who they think they are either; they better not play around with me. I'll show them who in the hell they're playing with. They'll find out fast that they aren't fucking with any boy when they fuck with me. I'll put my foot in their ass quick. Once I get started on them, I'll fix their ass up right. I've ruined more than one good man in my time, and Jack, I'll do it again too. That's the way I am, and that's the way I'll be until the day that I die. Everybody knows that's the way I am.

INCIPIENTLY VIOLENT SELF-IMAGES

Incipiently violent self-images also have two hallmarks, one of which they share with violent self-images and the other of which they do not. First, as in the case of violent self-images, the individuals are seen by others and see themselves as having violence-related personal attributes as a *salient* characteristic. In contrast to people with violent self-images, however, these individuals are seen by others and see themselves as having an *incipiently violent disposition,* that is, *only* a willingness or readiness to make serious threats of violence, such as violent ultimatums and menacing physical gestures, toward other people.

The essential difference between violent self-images and incipiently violent ones is that in the former the individual is viewed by others and views himself as definitely and genuinely being violent, whereas in the latter this is still highly problematic. Neither the individual nor others have determined with any certainty whether he may be "more show than go." Thus the verdict of others, and of the person himself, remains out with regard to his true violence potential. An example may make clearer the nature of an incipiently violent self-image. Case 28 illustrates a woman in her early forties who was convicted of criminal homicide and who held an incipiently violent self-image at the time of her offense.

Case 28: Criminal Homicide

I didn't care about anything. I let myself go completely. My appearance was bad. I didn't fix my hair, put on makeup, or care about my clothes. I wasn't attractive to men any more. I used ugly language and drank all the time. I couldn't do my job at home as a mother or at the place where I worked.

My boss knew my work wasn't as good as it used to be; he thought I was slipping. My work was sliding downhill bad. My husband saw me as an ugly old hag. He said I was just a piece of a woman because I had had a hysterectomy, and he had no more sexual desire for me. He and my oldest daughter both thought I was just a bitchy old woman and an alcoholic who made molehills into mountains. All of the kids felt that I was just an old crab who hollered all the time. I guess I was despicable.

I was a bitter and bad-tempered person. I couldn't accomplish anything, and nothing that I tried seemed ever to work out. I was full of hate. I wasn't desired by anybody, and my husband didn't have any attraction for me. I felt rejected and like a stupid fool for letting my husband mistreat me. I was getting fed up and easily angered by things. I made a lot of awful threats to people, but they thought it was mostly just big talk. Everybody thought that I would do little real action besides get drunk, scream and cuss, and throw things at people until I passed out.

NONVIOLENT SELF-IMAGES

Nonviolent self-images are marked more by what is absent than by what is present. The people are not seen by others and do not see themselves as having a violent or an incipiently violent disposition. They furthermore are not seen by others and do not see themselves as having violence-related personal attributes as a salient characteristic. To the contrary, in these self-images the people are seen by others and see themselves as having as their *salient* characteristics a blend of both positive and negative—although all nonviolence related—personal attributes, such as goodhumored or dour, outgoing or shy, lazy or industrious, personable or boring, obnoxious or polite, ugly or attractive, smart or stupid, and so on. Unsurprisingly this was the rarest of the types of self-images found among the violent offenders. Case 48 illustrates a woman in her early twenties who was convicted of aggravated assault and who held a nonviolent self-image at the time of her offense.

Case 48: Aggravated Assault

I was a young and serious-minded married woman and a perfect lady. People thought I had class. I wore fine dresses and minks, gold rings, and was a singer in my man's band. My girlfriend who sang with me saw me as a beautiful person. She thought my personality was nice and that I was a pretty, cat-eyed broad who could really catch dudes' eyes, but she knew I didn't play that game. The dudes in the band saw me as a beautiful person too. They thought that I was sexy, and they considered me a good singer. They knew that I could socialize with people real good and felt that I was real nice to work with. They thought that I was a classy broad.

My husband thought that I was a young and pretty woman and real good to get down with since he said that I had a pussy as tight as a little baby. In fact, he more or less thought of me as innocent because I hadn't learned all the ropes yet, but he still thought that I had a lot of sense for my age. He considered me a pretty good wife, and he knew that I had enough class for him to take me anywhere. I was intelligent and a good conversationalist and hostess. He knew that I didn't bite my tongue about anything either. I spoke my mind. I just wanted to have a family, be a mother, and live a nice life. I felt like a lady and wanted to be treated like a lady, but my husband was getting crazy and then embarrassing me in front of everybody behind his jealousy.

NOTE

1. Typologies of violent offenders have been made on other bases besides their self-images. Some recent examples are Cole, Fisher, and Cole's (1968)

typology of the "personality styles" of "murderesses" as masochistic, overtly hostile violent, covertly hostile violent, inadequate, psychotic, and amoral; Megargee's (1966, 1965) division of violent offenders into "undercontrolled and overcontrolled personality types;" and Toch's (1969) typology of violence-prone personalities as self-image promoting, self-image defending, reputation defending, pressure removing, exploiting, bullying, self-defending, self-indulging, norm enforcing, and catharting. The common theoretical rationale underlying these typologies is that violent individuals always have some type of abnormal or deficient psychological makeup that causes them to commit violent criminal acts. The interpretations of situations that the individuals make when they commit violent criminal acts are either totally ignored or treated as completely predetermined by their abnormal or deficient psychological makeups. Thus this theoretical rationale is completely contrary to the one I use here.

7 Self as Object and Process: The Linkage between Self-Images and Interpretations

According to the interpretive approach, an individual's self-image should be congruent with the interpretations that he forms of situations that confront him. An individual judges the situations that confront him and other people's opinions of him from the attitudes or standpoints of his generalized other. Since people construct their self-images and their interpretations of situations from a common standpoint, or with the same yardstick, their self-images should match their interpretations.

In the fifty-eight cases at hand, I discovered that the types of self-image that the offenders held at the time of their offenses were always congruent with the types of interpretation that they formed of the situations in which they committed the violent criminal acts. More fully, individuals who held nonviolent self-images committed their violent criminal acts only in situations in which they formed physically defensive interpretations. Those holding incipiently violent self-images committed their violent criminal acts only in situations in which they formed physically defensive interpretations or frustrative-malefic ones. Finally, those holding violent self-images committed violent criminal acts in situations in which they formed malefic, frustrative, frustrative-malefic, or physically defensive interpretations.

The invariant link I found between nonviolent, incipiently violent, and violent self-images and the various types of interpretations can be illustrated by examples of the perpetrators' self-images in conjunction with their interpretations of situations in which they committed violent criminal acts. Case 5 represents a man in his early twenties with a nonviolent self-image and the physically defensive interpretation that he formed of the situation in which he committed an aggravated assault.

Case 5: Aggravated Assault

Self-Image

My family thought I was a hard worker who provided exceptionally well. They knew that I was highly motivated, a person who wanted to learn. I believed you could get anything you wanted if you knew something and knew it well. I knew you had to have a bill of goods to sell. People saw me as a guy who knew a trade and knew it well. I could sell myself anytime. I always had something to offer. I would sell an image of doing a great job when I was only working up to one-half of my potential. It was a shortcut way to get the most. I had my own style.

I loved self-accomplishment. I was a perfectionist. I wanted to make it before I was forty, make it while I was young; that was what I tried to do. I thought I had done it. I had pride in myself.

People saw me as Mr.————. I was a neat dresser. I loved money and what it would buy to an extreme people didn't realize. I liked luxury, $200 suits, diamond rings, gold watches, new, fancy cars. There was nothing else. That was where it was at. I was hip to what was happening. Nobody could get an angle on me.

Interpretation

X and I were getting a divorce, and my lawyer advised me to move out of the house. I went home to get some of my things out of the basement.

I heard X coming down the steps while I was packing my stuff to leave and first glanced at her when she was at the middle of the steps. I figured she was coming down to talk, but when she didn't say a word to me, I stopped packing and turned toward her. I saw that she had a boning knife. I thought that she was trying to steal me, stab me on the sly, while my back was turned. I jumped over a box into the corner, and she started coming fast, fast, fast. I knew she was going to try to kill me. I took the gun from the bag that I had just packed and fired.

Case 57 represents a man in his midthirties with an incipiently violent self-image and the frustrative-malefic interpretation that he formed of the situation in which he committed a criminal homicide.

Case 57: Criminal Homicide

Self-Image

I was a good provider for my family and a hard worker. My boss considered me a much better than average employee. He thought that I was a reliable, loyal, and honest worker. Many customers even called and said how nice and polite a driver that I was. I got along good with everybody. My boss knew that I was a very reserved individual and never said anything out of the way to people.

My wife thought that I was boring and a narrow man because my interests and time were completely monopolized by sports and TV. It disgusted her that all I wanted to do was come home, take my shirt off, sip on a beer, eat, and watch TV and then go to different sports events on the weekends with my kids. The kids always had fun doing it. The sports world was all that I liked, and I had nothing to say that didn't have something to do with it. I didn't care for any intellectual-type things, and my wife knew it. She also called me antisocial, but I always got along good with all the people that I came into contact with. I just didn't want any intimate after-hours relationships with any of them. I didn't care about things like friends coming over.

My wife thought that I was physically unattractive too. She said I was a slob because I wouldn't keep myself neat and clean and dressed up. When I came home from work, I was tired and wanted to relax. I didn't feel like shaving and showering and changing right away like she wanted. She thought that I was a poor husband, period.

She said that I was too rigid and bossy. She felt that I forced her to accept all my decisions with threats about what I would do if she didn't. I know I sure frightened her when I got mad because I did let her know that she better damn well accept my decisions and not complain about it too much. I was a hardworking man, a good provider, and generous to my family, so there shouldn't have been any complaints from her about who gave the orders, what I did, and the rest. But I still had to let her know from time to time that she better not take her crap too far.

Interpretation

I was out of town, and I called my wife one night to check on what was going on at home. She told me that she had seen an attorney and was filing papers to divorce me. I asked her to hold off until I got back home and could sit down and talk it over with her, but she said, "No, this time I really mean it." After she told me that, I blew up and said, "You better not do that to me. If you do, you'll be sorry for it." She said, "I had a restraining order placed on you, so if you come around here bothering me, the police will get you." I said, "If I really want to get you, the police can't save you." I thought that telling her that would scare her, but it didn't. She just acted calm and confident, like she had everything all planned out. That got me madder. I knew then that it was no use raising any more hell over the phone since it wasn't intimidating her. I figured that I had to get home and confront her face to face. I just felt plain mad. I hung up the phone and headed straight for home. I wanted to see if she would talk as brave about a divorce to me when I got home as she did over the phone.

When I did get home three hours later, she was in bed, asleep. I woke her up and told her to get up, that I wanted to talk. I told her if she stopped with the divorce that I would promise to act better and . . . but she wouldn't buy any of it. I got angrier and angrier. Then she came out and said, "Look, please do me this favor and give me a divorce." At that moment I felt cold hatred for her inside me. I told myself that I better leave before I exploded on her, but then I decided the hell with it, and I looked at her straight in the face and said, "Well, X, you better start thinking about those poor kids of ours." She said, "I don't care about them; I just want a divorce."

My hate for her exploded then, and I said, "You dirty, no-good bitch," and started pounding her in the face with my fist. She put her arms up and covered her face, so I ran and got my rifle and pointed it at her. I said, "Bitch, you better change your mind fast or I'm going to kill you." She looked up and said in a smart-ass way, "Go ahead, then; shoot me." I got so mad and felt so much hate for her that I just started shooting her again and again.[1]

Case 29 illustrates a woman in her late twenties with a violent self-image and the malefic interpretation that she formed of the situation in which she committed an aggravated assault.[2]

Case 29: Aggravated Assault

Self-Image

I would have been best described as a "femme fatale." Many men were sexually attracted to me, and I was sexually attracted to many different men. The men that I knew saw me as a sweet, cute, and sexy woman who loved to party, and they knew that I was loose too. But I was unsure about myself. I was an emotionally unstable person. I would usually act nice and be sweet, but I could get really hateful too. Once I did get real mad, I blew it, and I would do anything to somebody. Some people realized that when I went crazy, I was dangerous.

My old man thought I had a delicious body and was a good baller, but he called me a chump and a whore a lot of times. He knew I liked to run around, go bar hopping, get myself loaded or drunk and ball. My girlfriends knew that I liked to sneak around too. I did love sex, all kinds, and a whole lot of it. I was a nymph—so what?

I was also a top waitress. I kept a clean house, and I cooked good and tried to be a good mother to my kids too, although I felt guilty sometimes for not spending more time with them.

Interpretation

My boyfriend and I were bickering when he announced to me that he had decided to go back to his wife and was going to pack his bags and leave. He said that now that he had a job making good money, she would take him back, and that he thought that they could make it together. I said, "Then you better give me some money for living here the last two months free and pay me back all the money that I've loaned you too." He said, "I don't owe you a damn penny for living here, and I don't have to pay you back any of that money you gave me." I said, "You dirty SOB, you don't give a damn about me. You've just been using me all along, haven't you?" He didn't give me an answer; he just acted cool and ignored me. I said to myself, "He can't get away with pulling this after all the things that he has already done to me. He broke up my relationship with X; he lived here free; he took my money, ruined my car. . . . He has just done too much to me to get away with it." I said, "Don't think that you are going to get away with this that easy," and he just got up and said he was packing his things. Then I started thinking about what I could do to get him. Poison him? No, he's not going to want to be eating anything now. I guess I have to shoot him. Then I thought I better not because I'd get into a lot of trouble for it, but finally I told myself, "Enough is enough; I'm going to do it. I don't care if I do get in trouble." While I was still worked up and had the nerve, I went and got the pistol that my old boyfriend had left in the house. Then I walked up to him and said,

"You dirty rotten SOB." He said, "Please don't shoot me." I said to myself, "You yellow punk, you never stopped beating me when I asked you," and I shot him.

Finally, case 9 illustrates a man in his late twenties with a violent self-image and the frustrative interpretation that he formed of the situation in which he committed a forcible rape.

Case 9: Forcible Rape

Self-Image

Most people thought I was a good guy who always took care of his family and was a good provider and worker. I was loved by most everybody—my wife, kids, in-laws, and the guys I went around with. My father-in-law said that I was the best son-in-law that he had. They all liked me because I joked and laughed a lot.

They knew that I was a happy-go-lucky guy who minded my own business, but they knew that I was a man, and when I got to drinking, look out. You couldn't tell me anything. I did what I wanted no matter what it took. I was a crazy lunatic then and got real mean. My wife would get scared of me when I was drinking, too, because I would hit her one time too many. Everybody said that alcohol made me become a lunatic. I know that it got me twenty years.

I was a real man who liked to gamble around, do some drinking, and search for pussy. I was a searcher, married or single. What women got, their curves and shapes, I liked and needed. I would take it any way that I could. I didn't like anybody interfering with my getting pussy. I'd beat them good if they did. I was a pussy raper. I believed in taking pussy by my might or whatever else it took to get it.

If I had twenty girls, I'd fuck every one of them. I got tired of sex with one woman. I knew a man could go out, search and take pussy, and not lose his respect. I believed a man has the right to a woman's beauty. When I saw it, I wanted it. I liked to be the first man to top a new pussy to boot. Pussy was always on my mind. The guys I went around with knew it, and they looked for it too. I was a searcher, a real man, and a good fucking guy.

Interpretation

I hadn't had any pussy for some time, so I felt horny as shit. Then I started thinking about this girl I met at a party a couple of weeks ago. She was built thin, but enough meat was on her to throw it up to me good. She never acted interested in me, but I had heard that her and the older woman in her building were giving up boatloads of pussy. I was drunk and my mind was on pussy, so I headed for their place. (I found out from a friend where they lived.) When I got there, I noticed the older woman in her room with the door wide open, so I went in and said, "Hi." She asked me what I wanted. I said I wanted sex and decided to try to talk her into fucking first. But she said, "I'm not going to do anything like that with you," so I knew then I was just going to take it. I said, "Yes, you are," and beat on her, but she still wouldn't give open, so I got the pipe which she had next to her door. After I busted her once upside the head, she said, "Well, if that's the way you want to be about it, then you are going to have to take my clothes off yourself." I pulled her panties down and said, "Now bend over and spread open, before I bust you upside the head again, but even harder." When she bent over, I saw her big, old fat ass. I tried to drive my dick into her dark, brown spot, but it was too tight. I kept pushing and pushing, but my dick started going down on me. While I was trying to stick my dick up her, the younger woman that lived in the same building came home. The older woman said, "What you need is a taste of that young stuff, not me." I thought, "She's right about that," 'cause her stinking, ugly old ass wasn't doing nothing for me.

That young girl's pussy was what I needed. I'd been dreamin' about fucking her skinny, bony ass for some time. I pulled up my drawers and headed straight for her room across the hall. I kicked her door open. As soon as I saw her, I got hard again. When she asked me what I thought I was doing, I said right out front, "I want to fuck you." She said, "Get out, get out of here." I got mad and grabbed her around the collar, but she started screaming, "Rape, rape, rape. . . ." I told myself, "I am going to do whatever I got to do to get that pussy." I started squeezing her neck and saying, "Shut up, shut up. All I want is some pussy; I don't want to hurt you." She broke away from me and went into the kitchen, where she got a knife and cut me. I finally knocked the knife out of her hand, but she slipped past me and got out the door. When I heard her run out the building into the street hollering at the top of her lungs "Rape, rape, rape . . . ," I thought, "I am in real fucking trouble now."[3]

As all these cases demonstrate, the self-images of violent criminals are always congruent with their violent criminal actions. Nonetheless psychiatrists, such as Emanuel Tanay (1972), have argued that the typical violent crime is an "ego-dystonic" rather than an "ego-syntonic" act. Ego-syntonic acts are acceptable to the ego and thereby congruent with an individual's self-image. Conversely, ego-dystonic acts are unacceptable to the ego and thereby incongruent with an individual's self-image. Thus if violent crimes were in fact ego-dystonic, then the self-images of the violent criminal actors would be at sharp odds with their violent criminal actions instead of being consistent with them. Although violent criminal acts may be ego-dystonic for psychiatrists, they are ego-syntonic for the people who commit them.

In short, people with nonviolent self-images commit substantially violent criminal acts only on the basis of physically defensive interpretations, and those with incipiently violent self-images do so only on the basis of physically defensive or frustrative-malefic ones, whereas people with violent self-images do so on the basis of any of the four types of interpretations identified here.[4] Thus people with violent and incipiently violent self-images interpret a wider range of situations as calling for violence on their part than do those with nonviolent ones, which further underscores that their self-images are congruent rather than incongruent with their violent criminal actions.

NOTES

1. In keeping with the subject's wishes, case 57 is not presented here in its entirety.

2. For another illustration of an individual with a violent self-image and the malefic interpretation that he formed, see case 35 in chapters 4 and 6.

3. In the original edition I stopped the presentation of case 9 at the point where the subject reported that "I got the pipe. . . ." In note 1 of chapter 4 I explain my reasons for excluding this material from the original and for including it in this edition.

4. A likely exception might be people who commit serious violent acts only during isolated moments of their lives, such as riots. Unfortunately no people with these experiences could be found for interviews.

8 Careers of Violent Actors

According to the interpretive approach, a career is a selective life history in which are recorded the major changes that people make in their selves and actions over all or some span of their lives. The individual's past momentous actions and former relatively stable self-images are excavated for the purpose of plotting the path that his life has followed in reaching its present destination.

To plot these paths I gathered data on the careers of thirty-five of the violent offenders. I did this by asking them two sets of questions. The first set of questions dealt with their self-images. I asked the offenders how they saw themselves at the time of their offense; how they thought others saw them during that time period; whether these others saw them correctly and why; and how long, or between what approximate ages, they saw themselves and thought others saw them in this way. The second set of questions dealt with the offenders' past violent criminal actions. I asked them to describe all the past violent acts that they had perpetrated during the period of their lives when they held the self-image just described. I also asked them to note the degree of injury that they inflicted on the other person, approximately how old they were when they committed the act, and whether the police contacted them with regard to it.

I then asked the offenders the same sets of questions for an *earlier* time of their lives *ending* with the time period when they held the self-image and committed the violent criminal acts previously described. These two sets of questions were repeated for still earlier time periods of the offenders' lives until the subjects could no longer provide answers to the questions about their self-images. When this point was reached in the questioning, they said to me such things as "To tell you the truth, I don't remember much about how I saw myself or how other people saw me back then," or "Before that I saw myself as just another kid, and I guess everybody else saw me as just a kid too; that's about it."

My study of these data reveals several critical features of violent careers. First, the self-images these offenders held over their lives fall into the same basic types previously identified—violent, incipiently violent, and nonviolent. Second, the periods of their lives when they held these types of self-images also fall into three types—*substantially violent, unsubstantially violent,* and *negligibly violent.*

Substantially violent periods are marked by the commission of one or (usually) more substantially violent acts that was not victim precipitated or committed as a result of forming a physically defensive interpretation. Substantially violent acts have either of two qualities. (1) The perpetrator inflicted a substantial physical injury; that is, he deliberately injured the victim either fatally or to a degree that usually calls for a physician's attention, such as results from a shooting, stabbing, clubbing, or relentless beating. (2) The perpetrator substantially sexually violated the victim, as in the case of coitus, sodomy, fellatio, or cunnilingus under either the threat of substantial physical injury or the infliction of substantial or unsubstantial physical injury.

Unsubstantially violent periods are marked by the commission of several unsubstantially violent acts but no substantially violent ones that were not victim precipitated. Unsubstantially violent acts have either of three qualities. (1) The perpetrator inflicted unsubstantially physical injury; that is, he deliberately injured the victim to a degree that usually does not call for a physician's attention, such as results from being slapped, backhanded, pushed, or mildly punched, choked, or kicked. (2) The perpetrator unsubstantially sexually violated the victim; that is, he violated her to a degree short of coitus, sodomy, fellatio, or cunnilingus. (3) The perpetrator did not inflict substantial physical injury but did seriously threaten the victim with such injury, as in the case of verbally threatening to injure someone while displaying or discharging a dangerous weapon when substantial sexual violation does not take place.[1]

Finally, negligibly violent periods are marked by the commission of no substantially and few, if any, unsubstantially violent acts that were not victim precipitated.

The third critical feature of violent careers that my study of these data reveals is that the type of self-images the offenders held over their lives is correlated with the type of violent periods they had. More fully, when the perpetrators held violent self-images, they underwent substantially violent periods. When the perpetrators held incipiently violent self-images, they underwent unsubstantially violent periods. Finally, when they held nonviolent self-images, they underwent negligibly violent periods. I illustrate this correlation in the examples that follow.

Last, my study of these data discloses that the careers of violent offenders fall into three basic types: *stable, escalating,* and *de-escalating.*

STABLE VIOLENT CAREERS

In the first type of career that offenders have, a stable career, the individual has the same type of self-image and violent periods over his entire life. Within this type of career, two subtypes can be identified: *stable violent* and *stable nonviolent.* In the former subtype the individual's self-images and violent periods were always violent and substantially violent, respectively; in the latter they were always nonviolent and negligibly violent, respectively.

Although only two subtypes of stable careers are identified here, a third possibility can be easily contemplated: a stable marginally violent one. There were no empirical grounds for differentiating this particular subtype of stable career, however, because no one was found whose self-image and violent periods were always incipiently violent and unsubstantially violent, respectively. This suggests that incipiently violent self-images and unsubstantially violent periods may be more transitory than the other types. People who are in unsubstantially violent periods of their lives and hold incipiently violent self-images apparently begin perpetrating substantially violent acts and develop violent self-images, or else they stop perpetrating unsubstantially violent acts and develop nonviolent self-images. Of course, it makes sense that these individuals must either stop making threats and attempts to seriously injure or sexually violate other people or actually carry out these threats and attempts, because other people will probably challenge them to do so sooner or later. An individual can bluff people only for so long before his bluff is called.

Case 56 illustrates the stable violent career of a man who was convicted of criminal homicide.

Case 56

Age 9–14: Violent Self-Image

I was very mature and perceptive beyond my years, and I had a lot of freedom. I went backpacking and camped out by myself regularly. I knew the realities of life too. I always had chores around the house, and I did them. I also always did odd jobs after school to earn my own spending money, and I worked at odd jobs all summer long. I believed at a young age that a person should work for what he gets. I was super-intelligent and a bold kid too. I would often manipulate grown-ups to my advantage without them even knowing it, and I had gotten drunk several times. I was very mischievous but not offensive where grown-ups were concerned. My folks considered me to be a real good kid.

I had a little temper too, and after my grandfather taught me how to fight, I was the cock of the walk at school. I believed in always standing my ground, but not to push people off theirs. I was proud that there were kids sixteen and seventeen who wouldn't fuck with me. I tried to follow the code of fair play and fighting that my grandfather instilled in me: "It is worse to win a fight if you're wrong than to get your ass whipped if you are right. But if you are right, then no holds are barred. If fists don't work, then don't box. Pick up a rock, baseball bat, anything. A bully doesn't deserve a boxing match anyway, but anything that he gets." I didn't always follow this since sometimes I was the bully, but I always kept in mind that a man should have whatever he asks for. Everybody knew that I would really fight, and when I got into a fight, I didn't ever play. I would fistfight or do whatever else was needed to win.

Age 9–14: Substantially Violent Period

Age 9: Substantially Violent Act. I came home from school with my knees all skinned up and my trousers ripped. My grandfather asked me what happened. I told him that a big black kid beat me up at recess. He said that he didn't want any nigger beating up his grandson and then began giving me boxing lessons. I jumped the kid the next day at recess, but he downed me again. When I told my grandfather about it, he whipped me and then told me that I better beat that kid's ass the next day or he was going to whip me even harder. I knew that kid couldn't hurt me as much as my grandfather could, so I tried to whip his ass again. I fired on him at recess and hit him as hard as I could in the face and downed him. While he was down, I kicked him in the head and face good and hard and bloodied his mouth and broke his nose. Then I took his place at school after that as the cock of the walk. I was sent home from school that day. [No police.]

Age 11: Substantially Violent Act. I started a bad fistfight with this kid a lot older than me. After we exchanged maybe a dozen hard punches, I wanted to quit. I told him that I wanted to throw in the towel, but he wouldn't stop punching me. Finally I broke and ran, but he started running after me. So then I really got mad and stopped and picked up a large stone and busted him in the head. I opened up his forehead bad and he needed ten stitches. [No police.]

Age 12: Substantially Violent Act. This guy followed me and my friend to my house after school. We were in front of an old shed in my backyard when he picked a fight with my friend. I told the guy to get out of my yard, but he wouldn't leave, so I punched him in the face. He then got mad and picked up a wagon axle and told me to keep out of it. I decided then that I was still going to get him out of my yard, so I grabbed a steel pipe out of the shed and swung it at him as hard as I could. It knocked the axle that he was holding out of his hand and then hit his arm and broke it. I didn't get into any trouble behind it. [No police.]

Age 13: Substantially Violent Act. Two guys and I were playing darts out back of my house. I told them both that they had better not throw any darts at the house since I had gotten into trouble behind doing it, but one of the guys did it anyway. I picked up a two-by-four and told him that he better not do it again. He did, and I got mad and hit him as hard as I could in the face with it. I broke his nose, and he got stitches in the face. [No police.]

Age 14: Substantially Violent Act. We had just finished supper, and my stepfather told my brother to wash the dishes, but he refused. My stepfather was drunk, and he started throwing dishes off the table. My mother tried to clear the table before he broke all the dishes, and he smacked her in the face. My brother got up and ran for the back door, but my stepfather cut him off and told him not to leave the kitchen. My mind was on getting out of there as fast as I could before he got on me. I got up from the table, but he pushed me back down in my chair and said, "You better not move from that chair until I tell you, or I'll beat your ass good just like I did on your birthday." My mother and brother cleared the dishes left on the table and started washing them. He just stood there glaring at us until the dishes were done. Then he told us all to go into the living room. He bolted the front door shut, and my brother turned on the TV. My stepfather then turned it off so hard that he broke the knob clean off, and he began yelling at my brother again about the dishes. Finally I asked my stepfather if I could please go to my room and lay down since I wasn't feeling well. He told me it was okay, so I went to my room.

A couple of minutes later he came into my room and said, "You know, you're damn lucky you're sick, because you were the one who should have done those dishes." Then there was a crash in the living room, and he ran in there and checked it out. My baby brother had knocked over a lamp, and my stepfather smacked him for it. My baby brother started crying, and my stepfather told my mother, "You better shut that little bastard up." The fear of him that I felt inside then turned to cold hate and anger. The thought came in my mind to kill him. My .22 rifle then flashed in my mind. I got frightened just at the thought of it. I told myself that tonight I was going to kill him.

My mind turned back to my rifle. My stepfather had taken the bolt out of it and put it in his dresser drawer. I just sat there on my bed and tried to figure out a way that I could get into his room without him catching me. Then my mother said, "X, go get the baby's pacifier off the green dresser in my room." I hesitated. The thought of actually going into their room where my rifle bolt was scared me. My stepfather then yelled, "Didn't you hear your mother, boy? Go get that pacifier." I walked into their room. First I got the rifle bolt out of his drawer. I put it in my pocket and pulled out my shirt to cover it. Then I got the pacifier and went into the living room. When I walked by my stepfather to give my mother the baby's pacifier, I trembled, and he noticed it and thought that it was from fear of walking by him, but it was mostly from the rifle bolt and what I had in my mind to do. My looking scared must have satisfied him good because he told me that I could go back to my room and rest.

As soon as I did, I put the bolt in my rifle and got some shells out of my sock drawer. As I loaded the rifle, I started thinking about what would happen if I fired and missed him and what would happen if I shot and killed him. I wondered if I'd go to prison. Finally I decided that I should kill him, so I grabbed my rifle and walked into the hallway and then turned around and walked back into my room. I did this over and over again until finally I got up enough nerve to walk into the living room. My stepfather was sitting on the sofa. I pointed my rifle straight at him and just stood there looking at him. Finally he noticed me, and he jumped up, and I pulled the trigger. I got him in the side, and he fell back down on the sofa. I felt relieved. He looked up at me, and I pulled the trigger again. This time I hit him in the neck, and his whole body started quivering, and I pulled the trigger again and got him in the head. He then completely collapsed down on the floor. I felt tranquil. I knew that he was dead. I had to go to the school for boys behind it.

Age 14½–19: Violent Self-Image

Everybody at the school for boys knew that I had a murder beef, so they were scared of me. Since it was accepted that I could whip anybody's ass there, I was the duke of the cottages. I ran all the fucking cottages, and everybody, including the supervisors, knew it. I got the privileges of the rank and I enjoyed them. I was a little con artist too. I mixed my earlier code about fighting with a new attitude that thieving was all right.

When I left the boys' school, I was a headstrong, wild, and reckless kid. I was game for anything that would make me a lot of money quick. I drove around all over the place robbing and stealing, and I got involved in a lot of harebrained schemes. People saw me as a John Dillinger–type gangster. I had balls and would do things that a person in his right mind just wouldn't do. I was insane. I drank too much and got way out of line, and if anybody tried to stop me, I'd jump right on them. I usually packed a pistol and would take a shot at a sucker in a minute. I also was an instinctive marksman, so if anybody did provoke me, I was subject to blowing off their goddamn head. Everybody who knew me thought I could seriously hurt or shoot and kill somebody.

Age 14½–19: Substantially Violent Period

Age 16½: Substantially Violent Act. I hadn't been out on parole from my murder beef too long when I got into a hassle with four dudes at a drive-in. This dude came up to my car and started talking smart to my date. I told the punk to beat it, and he came over to my side of the car and cussed at me through the window and told me to try and make him beat it. Then I saw his partners start heading over to my car. I decided to give them what they needed, and I grabbed a hammer that I kept under the front seat and jumped out. I hit one of them square in the head and downed him. The two others then went for me, and I cracked one over the shoulder and the other one in the head and downed both of them. The other dude with them then ran.

The police got me, but all the witnesses said that those other dudes started it for no reason, so they decided to drop the case against me. The three dudes that I hit went to the hospital in an ambulance. I fucked them up bad. I fractured one's collarbone and broke the other two's skulls open.

Age 17: Unsubstantially Violent Act. One night I was half-drunk and driving kind of slow down a narrow road when the driver behind me started tailgating and beeping his horn. I looked in my rearview mirror and saw that it was a carload of guys. I got pissed off and decided to slow down some more. When I turned off onto another road, they started following me, so I pulled over and got out of my pickup with my rifle. When they started pulling over their car, I fired several shots at them, and then they turned around and drove off fast. I didn't hit any of them, but I know that I did hit their car a few times. [No police.]

Age 18: Substantially Violent Act. I got into a hassle with a dude at a beer joint one night. He was being bounced out of the joint for getting too loud. I started laughing, and he got pissed off and downed me. He grabbed a beer bottle off the bar and hit me over the top of the head with it. I didn't need any stitches or anything, but I was hurting bad. I had a huge bump on the top of my head. When I finally got myself together, I went looking for him. Finally I drove around his house and noticed the lights were on. As I snuck up to his house, I saw him through a window and I fired my pistol at him several times. I then dead-headed to a gambling house and spent the rest of the night and next morning there with some tight partners of mine. The police arrested me for his murder, but there were no witnesses and I had a solid alibi, so they had to cut me loose.

Age 19: Unsubstantially Violent Act. I lived next to this guy whose dog barked all the time and woke me every morning. I told the man that he better shut his dog up, but he never listened. Then one morning when I had a terrible hangover the dog's barking woke me. I got mad, went out, and shot the dog dead. The guy came out screaming at me about the police and shit. I pointed my pistol at him and told him that if he didn't shut up that I was going to blast him too. He ran into his house, and I went back to my apartment, packed my clothes, and took off. I never did get arrested for doing it.

Age 19: Substantially Violent Act. I went over to this broad's pad that I knew. The two broads who shared the apartment with her and their boyfriends were there. Their boyfriends started a hassle with me behind my always coming over there drunk and offering the broads booze and shit. I told them that those broads were old enough to decide for themselves whether or not they wanted a drink or anything else. The big one then got mad and told me to beat it. I was half-drunk and in no shape to fight that big SOB, so I split. I went to a bar where I hung out and ran down what happened to some friends of mine there. I got all worked up about it and decided to go back over to the broads' pad. Two of my friends came along with me, and I sent one of them up to the door to tell the big dude that I wanted to see him outside. As soon as I saw him coming out, I grabbed the hammer from under my car seat. I got out when he came up to the car and hit him square in the head. He grabbed a hold of me as he fell down on his knees, and I smashed him in the head again. Then I hit him several more times in the body. I put him in critical condition, and his brain was damaged. I served ten years behind it.

Age 20–30: Violent Self-Image

Although I was born with better mental equipment than I had any right to expect (my IQ was measured at 137), I still occasionally did real dumb things that got me in big trouble. I was serving a sentence in prison these last ten years for something dumb that I did. But having to do all that time didn't make me a bitter person. I was more happy-go-lucky than most long-termers in the joint. I learned a good trade, had an uncanny skill at it, and got assigned good jobs because of it. I had a way of picking up on the right information and putting two and two together, so that I always knew what was coming down around the joint. In general I got along all right and was pretty happy in prison.

I could relate to most people in the place. I was tolerant of many styles and mixed with a variety of people. I had a lot of friends who didn't have anything positive for each other, but I handled it. I was a social chameleon. I hid or changed my true feelings as the occasion demanded. But most people in general trusted me. They knew I would do a guy a favor if I was in a position to. But I also could be a rotten SOB. I did some real rank things, but I also did some redeeming things over these years. I always identified with any underdog and hated bullies. I stepped in on occasion and took unnecessary risks to help out guys in bad situations by standing up for them and putting myself on the line for them.

I was respected by both institutional staff and inmates for the way that I conducted myself and handled my affairs. I was man enough to tell a guy to go get fucked, and I always dealt with people on a one-to-one basis. I expected them to do the same with me too. I didn't need any gang or clique to do my business for me; I was strong enough to handle it myself. If push came to shove, then I'd shove. I loved life, but I wasn't scared of death.

I was ready to kill or die, but I wasn't a stupid asshole about it. I didn't take any bullshit from anybody, but I didn't go out of my way to give it to people either. If I really got out of line, then I would say I was sorry. I didn't put myself on any serious crosses behind dumb bullshit. I knew when it was best to backpaddle and avoid trouble and when to stand up and meet it all the way. I established a heavy reputation around the joint, and it kept me from being picked out or stabbed behind any petty bullshit and let me have pretty much a free run.

Age 20–30: Substantially Violent Period

Age between Early Twenties and Thirties, Exact Age Withheld: Substantially Violent Act. During the ten-year stretch that I did in the pen for the ADW [assault with a deadly weapon], I only got into one hassle where something actually came down. I killed a dude behind ripping off a little kid who I really dug a lot. One cold dude kept putting pressure on this kid to get down with him. Finally the dude and his partners overpowered the kid and fucked him. When I found out what they did to him, I was pissed off, but I held my cool. A few days later I slid up behind the dude who planned it and shoved a shank all the way through his upper back and left it there. Then I quickly snuck away. Nobody even knew that the dude had been stabbed until over an hour later. Nobody saw me kill him, and I never advertised before or after it happened that I was out to get the guy, so I got away with it clean.

Case 37 illustrates the stable nonviolent career of a man who was convicted of criminal homicide.

Case 37

Age 14–17: Nonviolent Self-Image

I was dreaming about being a famous singer on stage with a band or being a famous basketball player. I was a wild and mischievous young dude. I liked to drink wine and cut it up with the other dudes, and sometimes I cut school. I also shoplifted some. I was having fun with the ladies, too. I was just young, dumb, and full of come. I was all right with the ladies as far as they were concerned, and I was concerned. Not too many of them ever rejected me. They thought I was a lover and sweet talker.

My steady girl thought that I was a nice-looking, attractive cat with a nice personality. I turned her on. She saw me as a nice, sweet dude. She thought that I had a good voice. The dudes at school knew that I was a better than fair young man with the ladies, and they considered me a good basketball player and thought I was a great singer. Everybody thought of me as a friendly cat who acted nice to people.

Besides my grandmother, all of my family thought that I was a nice, decent young man who respected people older than me. They knew that I didn't cause any trouble at home or at school. My grandmother disliked me when she was sober and hated me when she was drunk because she said that I wasn't my father's son. She mistreated me no matter what I did. I felt sorry for myself because I had to live with her and put up with her crazy shit.

Age 14–17: Negligibly Violent Period

Age 14: Unsubstantially Violent Act. A dude who always picked on everybody at school took my comb. I asked him to give me my comb back, and he told me to try and take it. When I reached for it, he punched me in the face. Then he said he was going to kick my ass good and started punching me all over. Finally I took my pencil out of my pocket and threatened to stab him with it. Then the teacher got us, and we were both sent home. [No police.]

Age 18–25: Nonviolent Self-Image

I liked to gamble, mainly shoot dice. I was crazy about music. I could sing all of the songs by Johnnie Taylor and Al Green. I was also woman crazy. Women considered me a handsome cat. I wasn't Rudolph Valentino, but I was a nice-looking and smooth-talking dude. I knew how to handle broads who had any type of personality, but I dug best broads who were fun-loving but quiet and clean physically and mentally. All the broads that I messed with thought that I was a good lover. They all let me know that I had a big dick and that I knew how to use it. Every woman that I ever gave some to said that I was large-sized. But they thought that I was a nice dude to spend time with out of the bed too.

The dudes that I ran around with knew that I got along good with the women. They considered me a player. They said that I was a pretty cool cat even though I was a country-ass nigger. They also thought that I was a cat with a good voice who could sing blues just like Johnnie Taylor. They saw me win enough money to know that I could shoot dice good too.

My people considered me a pretty fine young man who respected people older than him. They thought that I was a nice and courteous person. My father saw me as a young man trying to make it. He knew that I realized that I wasn't a child any more and that I had to make it on my own. He thought that I was man enough to take care of my own business and stay out of trouble.

I liked to have fun, but I liked to avoid trouble and troublemakers. I believed in respecting others, and I felt that I also deserved respect. I was a pleasant and good-humored dude. I tried to maintain a nice personality and a smile on my face. I could go for a joke. I didn't go around acting like any bad dude. I was a skinny-ass motherfucker, and I knew that I had to be a little cool about fucking with people. The dudes that I ran around with thought that I was a good dude who was easy to get along with, and so did the dudes that I worked with. I was a warm and free-hearted dude. I had feelings for people who were down and beaten. I'd do what I could to help a person. I'd share my last piece of bread with a hungry dude.

Age 18–25: Negligibly Violent Period

I was mugged once, but I never got into a fight where I jumped on somebody and shit.

ESCALATING VIOLENT CAREERS

In the second type of career that offenders have, an escalating career, the individual's self-image and violent periods become progressively more violent. On the basis of the degree of escalation exhibited, two subtypes of these careers can be identified: *fully escalating* and *partially escalating*. In the fully escalating subtype, actors' self-images and violent periods go from nonviolent and negligibly violent to incipiently violent and unsubstantially violent and finally to violent and substantially violent, respectively; in the partially escalating one, perpetrators' self-images and violent periods go only from nonviolent and negligibly violent to incipiently violent and unsubstantially violent, respectively. Case 34 illustrates the fully escalating career of a man who was convicted of aggravated assault.

Case 34

Age 12–16: Nonviolent Self-Image

People saw me as the average schoolboy who loved sports and things. I especially liked basketball, and my dream was to become the star player on the school team. Besides playing sports, I liked to build airplanes and talked about being an aeronautical engineer. My parents thought I was a good child. They liked it that I was heavy into aeronautics and sports. I didn't care about broads and running around. I was just content staying home around my family. The only thing that I ever did bad was stealing from my mother's pocketbook a couple of times. I guess I was what you would call a square kid.

Age 12–16: Negligibly Violent Period

I never had any real fights then. Once I got into a shoving match with a kid, but this fight was so light that it's not really worth talking about. No hard punches were even thrown. [No police.]

Age 17–19: Incipiently Violent Self-Image

I was a square dude then, but I hated school and shoplifted. My good partners who were up to my game knew that I was a good thief. The broads and dudes at school saw me as pretty cool. They thought that I dressed sharp and talked fast. Although I was popular, a few people at school who I didn't mingle with thought I acted too uppity and had a smart mouth. Most people at school thought I was a slick dude, but I wasn't considered bad. They knew I'd slap a broad's face in a minute, but I wouldn't jump on dudes.

My steady woman saw me as a cool and popular dude. She thought I had good looks, good conversation, and good tastes. She figured that I was a dude who was going to be something. She dug everything about me except for my always running after other tail. My nose was always open for pussy. I chased the broads. When she got mad at me, she also called me a coward and said I would slap and hit broads, but I was scared to hit dudes. I admit it.

My momma said that I was her baby, and she spoiled me. But she was still pretty hip to my game. She figured I was doing some thieving and said I was sneaky. She also knew that I was a fiend behind pussy and wasn't satisfied with my steady woman's hole. She called me a nasty, dirty little bastard because I was always smelling after women's tails and catching the clap all the time. She was right too.

Age 17–19: Unsubstantially Violent Period

Age 17–18: Unsubstantially Violent Acts. I got into four or five heavy arguments with my steady old lady where I had to slap or punch her a few times. She was a big and solid-built broad, and on two occasions I remember punching her once or twice in the face. On one of these occasions I busted open her lip, and on the other I bruised her cheek up. That's about all I did to her. [No police.]

Age 18: Unsubstantially Violent Act. This broad at school was going around talking dirt about me. When I heard about it, I told her she better stop running off that shit to everybody, but she kept it up. So I ran her down after school one day and slapped her in the mouth. Then I tore her blouse off, shoved her down on the ground, and took off. Shit, she didn't get hurt, just embarrassed. [No police.]

Age 19: Unsubstantially Violent Act. This broad who I was fucking on the side came over to my pad and said that she wanted to talk to my old lady about me. I told her to split but she wouldn't. When I started pushing her ass toward the front door, she put up a fight. So I hit the bitch with my fists in the face and bloodied her nose. Then my old lady ran into the room and jumped on the bitch too. As we pushed her out of the door, my old lady ripped her blouse off. [No police.]

Age 20–28: Violent Self-Image

I was a simple pimp and dope fiend. I just wanted enough money so I could lay back, relax, and stay high. I didn't want to work, period. I figured that I would never have anything working at any eight-hour-a-day job, but I could hustle women and make over a couple of hundred dollars a night. I wanted to have fine clothes and get a nice automobile the easy way. I considered myself a lover of women and was hung up behind getting new pussy. I thought that every foxy broad who walked down the street was a better fuck than the broads I had. I always had to check to see if they would dig on me. I was looking to be a big hustling pimp. People said that I had good looks, good conversation, and women enjoyed my company, and that's all you needed to be a pimp. I was dreaming of the day when I would have five or six hos [whores] and could just kick back and let them take care of me.

Street people, hustlers, dope peddlers, and other pimps considered me to be cool and accepted me as one of their own. They knew that I was no fool and gave me my respects. They knew if I had to get down, I would, so I didn't have to worry about anybody bothering my women. I was scared to get down with a man with only my hands, but I wouldn't hesitate to with a gun or knife, or if I could pick up something. My two old ladies who were with me the longest were scared to death of me. I would beat a woman's ass twice as fast as a man's. They knew that I'd whip their asses good in a minute. Shit, I believed in beating women's asses. One of them was scared that I might ruin her one day. If I got into a bad state of mind, I could kill somebody. When I came down off dope, my old ladies watched themselves because I got mad quick. They knew that I only loved myself and didn't care about anybody else and that I was good to be with when things were going good but hell to be around otherwise. But they still wanted me for their husband.

My people thought that I was doing what I pleased and trying to get everything that I possibly could from anybody, including them. They knew I was taking dope and hustling women. They said that I was no good to myself or anybody else. Shit, I didn't care what they said. I liked taking dope, hustling women, and acting bad. I enjoyed it all.

Age 20–28: Substantially Violent Period

Age 20: Substantially Violent Act. I was just hanging around outside of Tom's Bar one night when I spotted this fine-built middle-aged broad walking down the street by herself. I started following her. Along the way I picked up a short board, and when she passed by some empty garages, I fired on her. I busted her upside the head with the board and downed her. When I pulled her inside a garage, she started screaming, so I beat on her with my fists until she promised to shut up. After I made her give me some head, I took her jewelry and money and split. [No police.]

Age 21: Unsubstantially Violent Act. One of my women and I drove around looking for broads who were hitchhiking. We picked up a couple of hippie chicks and pulled off on a lonely road. I slapped and backhanded them in the face, and then we demanded all of their money. We searched both of them everywhere. We looked in their purses, pockets, bras, and panties. One of them tried holding out on us, so I gave her a couple of hard shots in the breast and stomach. [No police.]

Age 23: Substantially Violent Act. I had won over $600 gambling in a game behind a bar I hung out at. When I headed home with the money, two of the dudes who were there started following me. I picked up a large stone and waited for them to make their play. When they fired on me, I hit one of the SOBs in the head with the stone and downed him. The other one then busted me in the head with a jack handle and took my money. I had to go to the hospital and get fifteen stitches. [No police.]

Age 26: Substantially Violent Act. This dude who I had dealt a little dope with latched onto one of my hos. I went over to his pad to talk to him about it to see what he had to say. We got into a heavy argument behind it, and he said he was going to get his gun, so I knocked him down. Then I pulled out my knife and stuck him twice in the stomach. We started wrestling on the floor and I dropped my knife. When he got still, I noticed he was bleeding like a pig. I got scared he might die, so I rushed him to the hospital after he promised not to put the police on me. I then backtracked to his pad to jump my ho for causing me all of this trouble. I punched her in the face until she fell down. Then I kicked the shit out of her all over the head and body. I broke her nose, jaw, and some of her ribs. [No police.]

Age 27: Substantially Violent Act. My old lady came home unexpectedly one day and caught me getting down with another broad. She started screaming at us and going crazy. I told the broad that she'd better split because I had to straighten that bitch out. As soon as she left, I jumped into my old lady's ass good. I punched her in the arms, back, and face, and then I busted her head up against the wall five or six times. After that I just grabbed her ass by the shoulders and threw her right into the wall. She fell to the floor, and I kicked her in the stomach until she doubled up. When I finally finished with her ass, she had to stay in the hospital for a few days. [No police.]

Case 38 illustrates the partially escalating career of a man who was convicted of criminal homicide.

Case 38

Age 10–15: Nonviolent Self-Image

I was slick for my age. I hung out with a gang of older dudes and cut
school, played pool, and ran away from home. I was also into stealing and got booked for it when I was ten. Stealing was an everyday
thing for me then. I stole bikes, burglarized houses, and shoplifted
whiskey and wine to sell to older dudes. I loved stealing. It was ex-
citing, thrilling, and it gave me plenty of money to spend and made
me pretty independent. All my friends thought I was doing good.
They admired me for being a good thief. They knew that I could always get the goods and that I rarely got caught. I was known as such
a good thief that older dudes in the neighborhood were always after
me to steal something for them. They saw me just as a good thief.

My family thought I was a bad delinquent. But I wasn't a for-real
low rider or heavy gangster. I was into stealing and cutting school,
not fighting. I just didn't dig school or my home. I disliked the au-
thority of the teachers at school and of my father at home. I wanted
to get away from all that shit that teachers said at school every day
and that my father was talking at home. I just didn't like adults in
general, and I felt that the whole world was against me and my
friends.

Age 10–15: Negligibly Violent Period

Age 11: Unsubstantially Violent Act. I got into an argument with
another kid, and he hit me with his skate in the arm. I got mad and
bit his thumb. Neither one of us was really hurt. [No police.]

Age 16–19: Incipiently Violent Self-Image

I wanted to prove that I was a man, but I wasn't showy, and I didn't
try to draw attention to myself. I was always quiet and never spoke
just for the hell of it. I just didn't give a fuck and wanted to do what
I wanted. I was real independent from my family. I acted like a low
rider. I ran away from home and cut school, and I liked to smoke
weed, drop LSD and shoot pool, and talk about pussy. I also committed burglaries. I was a sneak thief, and I identified with the whole
low-rider trip.

The squares at school considered me an outcast. They knew that I
always cut school and got loaded and that I had gone to jail. They

thought that I was the type of dude who didn't give a fuck about anything. They thought that I always was tense and looked mean. They were leery of me.

My light and heavy partners considered me pretty cool and hip. They thought that I was all right, but too stubborn and bullheaded sometimes since I didn't like to take no for an answer. They all thought that I had a real hot temper because when I got mad, I'd threaten to kill people and shoot them and shit. But they didn't think that I would actually do it. They just knew that I was an explosive person, so you didn't fuck with me. My family thought that I was hot-tempered too and irresponsible. They knew that I was a thief and a low rider.

Age 16–19: Unsubstantially Violent Period

Age 16–18: Unsubstantially Violent Acts. I used to slap my sister around good and plenty, but I didn't ever seriously injure her. [No police.]

Age 17: Unsubstantially Violent Act. I was waiting at a bus stop next to some middle-aged man for the bus. When it came, he stepped in front of me and tried to get on the bus ahead of me, but I quickly jumped in front of him and stepped up onto the bus first. When I got to the top of the bus stairwell, he said some shit to me about pushing in front of him, and I turned around and told him, "Fuck you." He then started rushing up the steps of the bus door after me, so I kicked him hard in the chest twice and he fell down the steps of the bus. I then went to the back of the bus and sat down, and he got on the bus and started crying out to the bus driver. The bus driver said he wasn't getting into it, that it wasn't any of his business. Nothing else came down. [No police.]

Age 18: Unsubstantially Violent Act. I got into a light fight at the pool hall. These two dudes were playing eight ball, and I told one of them that I wanted to play a game or two, but he told me that I had to wait my turn like everybody else. I got mad because I didn't feel like waiting any longer, and I punched the dude hard in the mouth, but everybody rushed up and grabbed us right after I punched him, and that ended the fight. [No police.]

Age 19: Unsubstantially Violent Act. I was driving around in a friend's car when I saw this dude who I held a grudge against getting into a parked car. I was packing a .32, so I decided to shoot at

him a few times and scare the fuck out of him. I slowed down be-
side his car and fired four shots at him and fucked up his car real bad.
I got charged with doing it, but I wasn't convicted.

Age 19: Unsubstantially Violent Act. I was at a pool parlor in my
neighborhood when this white social worker came in who was
known as a snitch. I told him to get his white ass out of the place
because we didn't dig him being around, but he wouldn't leave, so I
finally swung the cue stick at him. He knocked the stick away with
his arm and then walked out. I swung the stick at him hard, but I
wasn't really trying to hit him. I just wanted to scare him good so he
would get the fuck out of the place. [No police.]

Age 19: Unsubstantially Violent Act. I got into a fight with X behind him not paying me back some money that he owed me. When
I asked him for the money, he said, "What money?" He outright denied that I ever loaned him any money. I got so mad that I felt like
killing him. I pushed him down and kicked him a few good times.
Then he suddenly remembered borrowing the money, and he told me
that he would pay me some back soon, so everything was cool. [No
police.]

Case 45 illustrates another partially escalating career of a man who was
convicted of criminal homicide.

Case 45

Age 14–18: Nonviolent Self-Image

I was a nice guy who got along good at home and at school. I wasn't
seen by my family or people at school as a goody-goody or a trou-
blemaker. I was friends with people who were both. Nobody thought
that I was tough, but they didn't think I was a chickenshit either.

I made out okay in school. I tried hard and did about average in
my studies, and I was a good athlete. People at school considered me
a hell of a track star. I didn't have to sit in the backseat to anybody
as far as my looks were concerned. I let my hair grow out, and with
it long the girls thought I was a real good-looking and cute dude. But
I didn't take full advantage of it since I didn't have enough confidence
in myself to act like a cool playboy. Secretly I was a sensuous motherfucker. I wanted to date all the girls in school and fuck them too,
but I just wasn't aggressive enough to meet them. I only expressed

my personableness around the girls that I knew and had talked to or else who I heard dug on me.

Age 14–18: Negligibly Violent Period

Age 16: Unsubstantially Violent Act. I took my steady girlfriend to a movie. Three guys came and sat near us. One of the guys who I knew said, "X, can't you do any better than that?" I ignored his remark at the time, but the next day I ran into him while I was caddying. I jammed him behind it and gave him a hard slap to the mouth. He didn't hit me back, so I just said, "Don't ever pull that shit again," and walked off, and that was the end of it. [No police.]

Age 19–21: Nonviolent Self-Image

I was a damn good salesman, and I was doing great at my job. In fact I had about the best sales job in the whole company where I worked. I could sell just about anything. I was very personable, and I could talk that sales shit. I loved the selling contests that the company regularly had because I always finished near the top. I was getting a lot of confidence in my ability to earn a good living selling. My boss considered me the top-dog salesman in the whole place since I always rolled in those sales. He thought that I was a together young man who was really going places. The other salespeople thought that I was doing good too. They saw me as a sharp salesman and as a ladies' man too. They were jealous because I made those commissions and got plenty of good pussy too. They knew that I had a stacked old lady and a cute little girlfriend on the side.

I had the world by the ass then. I was making plenty of money, drove a Grand Prix, acted cool, and fucked hard too. I was a wet and wild dude. I was hot in two beds, and I loved it. It was the best time of my life. I had my wife hanging on by her tits and had my girlfriend by her clit. My wife wanted to keep me, and my girlfriend wanted me to marry her.

My girlfriend thought that I was too much. She knew that I had a lot of things going for me. She thought that I had a good job, dressed sharp, and was a good-looking dude who acted cool. She even said that I was the hottest dude who ever laid her in a bed. My wife figured that I was living fast and wild, and she knew that I was playing around. She knew that I dressed way too sharp to be just going to work, and she was right. She thought I acted too cool and confident and arrogant.

She called me a finger snapper, a Casanova type who thinks he is a big, cool lover. I liked to get down with her, but she was shy and got to be a boring homebody. I just told her that I was old enough to go to town when I pleased and do what I pleased, and I did too.

Age 19–21: Negligibly Violent Period

I didn't have any real fights during this period. I got into arguments occasionally with my wife and girlfriend, but I never hit them.

Age 22–24: Incipiently Violent Self-Image

As far as work was concerned, I was doing great. I had established myself a reputation for being an outstanding salesman. I knew I could land a selling job anywhere and easily earn a good living. But as far as my home life, it was fucked up bad. I got divorced from my first wife and married my girlfriend. She felt I was a good salesman who would always have a good paying job, and she thought I could handle money well. She said I always dressed sharp, kept clean, and looked nice. I wasn't a slob, and I got down with her good.

But she also thought I was a fucked-up asshole, so she divorced me. Right after we got married she lost her respect for me. She said that I was a boring, nosy, possessive person with a wild temper. She felt that I was a bore because I just wanted to make love to her all the time. And she thought that I was nosy and possessive because I always wanted to know what she was doing and who she was doing it with. But I felt that I had a right as her husband to know about this shit. She said it was just jealousy, and she was scared where it might lead with my temper. I didn't go around blowing my temper every day, but I would get mad once in a while and smack her or threaten to beat the shit out of her to make her act right. She called me a woman hitter and said she hoped a dude would kick the shit out of me. Shit, I wasn't scared of dudes; I just didn't believe that a husband should put up with that crap from his wife.

Her family, of course, agreed with her. They thought that I wasn't a man but a dog that only wanted to fuck, threaten, and slap women around all day and sit on my ass. They resented me. But my family thought that I was a fool to put up with my second wife. They felt that she was going to do nothing but bring me trouble and that I better leave her. Shit, I was driven up the wall by her crap, but I wasn't able to cut her loose.

Age 22–24: Unsubstantially Violent Period

Age 22: Unsubstantially Violent Act. About 2:00 one morning I was in bed with my second wife when I got a horny nut. I woke her up, but she got indignant. I got mad because I really wanted to get down, so I slapped her in the face twice and shook her hard. She got mad at me, but it blew over quick. [No police.]

Age 22: Unsubstantially Violent Act. My second wife and I were driving to her parents' house on Christmas Day when we got into a heavy argument. I grabbed one of her arms and told her to shut up, and she scratched me. Then I really got pissed at the bitch and pulled the car off the side of the road and grabbed her in a heavy headlock. I told her that she better listen to me, but she wouldn't. She kept scratching me, and when I let her go, she ran out of the car. I chased down the crazy bitch, pushed her down, and pulled her back to the car. She wasn't really hurt, but her ears were reddened up good from the headlock that I put on her. [No police.]

Age 22: Unsubstantially Violent Act. Right after I had told my second wife not to ever be going any place with other dudes, I discovered that she did it. I was mad that she wouldn't listen to me, and I blew up. I started breaking everything in the house, the dishes, the clock, when I thought that I should get her and teach her dirty ass a lesson. So I punched her with my fists in the back two or three times and knocked the breath out of her. She threatened to call the police on me but never did.

Age 23: Unsubstantially Violent Act. After my second wife and I had separated, I heard that she had some dudes after me, so I started packing a pistol. One night when I walked out of a steak and eggs house, this dude jammed me in the parking lot and said, "Aren't you X?" I said, "Yeah, that's me, but who are you?" He said, "I heard about you." I said, "Man, I don't know what the hell you are talking about." Then he downed me with a punch and started kicking me. I pulled out my pistol and told him to back off quick. When I headed toward my car, he said, "Fuck your gun, punk" and walked toward me. I cocked the trigger on my pistol and said, "If you take another step, you dumb asshole, I mean it, I'll kill you." Then a friend of his said, "Stop, stop," and I got into my car and split. [No police.]

Age 24: Unsubstantially Violent Act. My second wife and I had been back together for about a week or so when we went to a pool party at our apartment building. I was drinking beer and having a mellow old time when I noticed her playing around with this single young dude.

I told her to cut that crap out, but later on I picked up on the body language that she was giving off to that dude. After I began watching her some more, I noticed that she was giving him the eye too, and the dude was tuned in on it. I tried to stay cool, but I felt that I shouldn't put up with that crap. She was living in my house and flirting with a dude like that right in front of me. That was it; I had had it with the dirty bitch. I took her in my apartment and asked her what the fuck she thought she was doing. I felt like she should get her ass kicked for doing that crap. I went into a rage and hit her with my fists twice in the ribs and pushed her down on the floor. Then I tore all the shades and shit down from the apartment and screamed at her. I didn't seriously injure her, but the next day she left me for good. [No police.]

DE-ESCALATING VIOLENT CAREERS

In the third type of career that violent offenders may have, a de-escalating career, the self-images and violent periods that an individual has had over his life become progressively less violent. On the basis of the degree of de-escalation displayed, two types of de-escalating careers can be identified: *fully de-escalating* and *partially de-escalating*. In fully de-escalating careers the individual's self-image and violent periods go from violent and substantially violent to incipiently violent and unsubstantially violent and finally to nonviolent and negligibly violent, respectively. In partially de-escalating careers, however, the self-image and violent periods go only either from incipiently violent and unsubstantially violent to nonviolent and negligibly violent or from violent and substantially violent to incipiently violent and unsubstantially violent, respectively.

Studies conducted at different times and places across the country have repeatedly shown that most violent offenders fall between the ages of fifteen and thirty.[2] Thus most violent offenders undoubtedly have either fully or partially de-escalating careers. I found only offenders with de-escalating careers among my participant-observation cases. Participant-observation case 2 illustrates the fully de-escalating career of a man in his late thirties who earlier in his life was arrested for aggravated assault.

Participant-Observation Case 2

Age 15–21: Violent Self-Image

I was the leader of X gang. I had a bad-ass reputation. I did some of everything—joy ride in stolen cars, take hubcaps, shoplift whiskey

and wine, crash parties, and run the streets chasing broads. I wasn't
known as a heavy thief because I eased back off stealing the big stuff—
the grand larceny raps. But I was known as one of the toughest dudes
on———Street. People around there knew that I was mean and liked
to fight. I didn't mind fighting at all. Either you were ready to fight
or you were a sissy punk who got kicked in the ass. I wasn't backing
down or running off from anybody. Everybody knew that I would get
down. I didn't believe in arguing with people; I'd push the button
on them. I'd fire on them and be done with it. When I got uptight, I
could explode. I would use my fists because I was fast and could box
good, but I wasn't scared to use a knife, chain, gun, or anything else.
I wasn't out to kill anybody, but if it had become necessary, I would
have. I wanted to be a bad motherfucker and not take any shit. I admired dudes who could kick ass.

Age 15–21: Substantially Violent Period

Age 15: Substantially Violent Act. I had a job at a car wash on the
weekends. One Saturday I got into an argument with this other dude
working there. I got mad, threw a bucket of water on him, and then
jumped on his ass. We started wrestling all over the floor, and the
other workers broke it up and told us to take it outside. When we got
outside, we started throwing punches. Then I knocked him up against
a wall and laid one punch after another on his face until the boss and
other workers pulled me off him. The boss couldn't stop the blood
coming from the top of both his eyes, and they had to rush him to
the emergency room, where he got a dozen stitches. I was fired. [No
police.]

Age 16: Substantially Violent Act. I was out for this dude's ass because he had broken the screen door at my house. We had almost gotten down before behind this, but it was broken up. Finally I heard he
was at this party nearby, and I went over there and called him outside.
We got to boxing in the street, and he tackled me. Finally I got back
up and caught him with a hard punch which bloodied his nose and
then another, but an even harder one which opened up his mouth.
After that he put his hands down and said he had enough. I said, "Fuck
you giving up," and kept beating on him like a punching bag until I
saw the police coming. His nose was broken, he got stitches in his lip,
and he lost a tooth. The police didn't catch up to me.

Age 17: Substantially Violent Act. My friends and I were out in
front of the barbecue pit we hung out at when these dudes came by

and said, "Motherfuckers, you better get the fuck out of here. If you don't, somebody's going to die." We shot back, "Eat it, punks." Then they said, "Motherfuckers, you're in trouble now," and started coming after us. We were carrying short swords that we had just stolen from the Masons, and when we pulled them out, those dudes broke and ran. We chased their asses, and I hit one of them over the head hard with my sword and dropped him. Blood was rushing out of the center of his head, and we got scared and split. I hurt that fucker bad. An ambulance came for him. [No police.]

Age 18: Substantially Violent Act. My friends and I were at a park drinking whiskey and quarts of beer when we got into an argument with these other dudes who drove up. All hell broke loose. I grabbed onto this dude, and he knocked me down and started choking me. Then I bit him in the thigh until I could taste his blood. He finally got my teeth out of him, but I got up and stomped him in the spine as hard as I could. Then the police drove up and everybody started running. I wasn't caught, but I hurt that dude bad. The police took him to the emergency room.

Age 20: Substantially Violent Act. My brother and I went to this party that a girl who lived behind us was giving. There were a lot of people there from other neighborhoods, and it wasn't too long before trouble broke out. This dude came up to me and jammed me behind some dumb bullshit. I wanted to have a good time so I passed it off. Then he went up to a friend of mine and jammed him too. After that he got back on my case. Finally I had had enough of the dude and told him to get out of my face or be ready to get down. He had a lot of partners at the party with him, so I slipped back home and got my pistol. When I returned to the party, everybody was outside. I fired two shots over the heads of the dude who had jammed me and his partners and told them to get the fuck going fast. But one of them yelled that I only had a blank gun. Then I got mad because they acted like I was bullshitting. Shit, I was serious. I was ready to shoot their fucking asses. I decided first come, first served. The first dude who took a step forward I shot. Nobody else pushed it, so I took off. An ambulance picked up the dude I shot, and I was later arrested and placed on probation for it.

Age 22–28: Incipiently Violent Self-Image

I was just the Joe Doe family man. I was married and had kids. My wife thought that I was a responsible young husband who worked hard every day and took care of his business. Besides [my] being too bossy, she considered me a good husband. She said that I was a hip dude because I liked to have fun and party. I had a high school education and worked hard, but I wasn't getting anywhere fast. I was nothing big, just a factory worker who was at the bottom of the plant. My friends around the neighborhood saw me as a young working married man who was into sports. Shit, my biggest kick was drinking whiskey and chasing it with beer. I was popular and outgoing and had a lot of friends. I was on baseball and football teams and played alleyball and shit with the other dudes. I was a good team member, and they thought I was one of the more decent athletes in the group.

They considered me a pretty bad dude in general, and so did the people around the plant. They knew that I could swell up real big and lay it out to people if they fucked with me. Once I got all mad, I'd tell a person, "I'll kick your goddamn ass if you don't back up." If I was really pushed hard behind something, I could get it on, but being married and having kids made me be slicker and wiser in dealing with people. I would put shit on them that I was going to do this and that, but not let it go. I tried to back them up without really getting it on.

Age 22–28: Unsubstantially Violent Period

Age 23–24: Unsubstantially Violent Act. A guy that I worked with at the plant was always bugging me while I worked by arguing with me about this or that shit. I warned him to cut it out, but he kept up this shit. Finally one day he took a potshot at me and said, "Why don't you just get your dumb fucking ass out of here?" I decided that I was going to set that dirty redneck straight. So I backhanded him across the face and said, "Don't ever fuck with me anymore." I also had to do this to another redneck around there for fucking with me too, about a year later. But I didn't injure either one of them bad or anything. [No police.]

Age 26: Unsubstantially Violent Act. My friend and I were at a football game, and we made some bets with the guys sitting behind us. We were drinking and bullshitting them when an argument broke out near the end of the game. We told them that we were going to kick their asses and shit if they didn't pay up. Finally, out in the parking lot I pushed one of the dudes down and kicked him in the back. A policeman came up and broke it up, but nobody was arrested. I don't think the dude I kicked was seriously hurt.

Age 27: Unsubstantially Violent Act. When I was walking out of the plant one day with my friends, this dude who I had just told to stop horsing around with me came up and gave me a play kick in the ass. It really humiliated me that he did that shit again right in front of my friends, so I jumped that motherfucker. I grabbed him around the throat and choked him, but I eased up just before I really hurt him and said, "Please don't ever do that shit again to me." [No police.]

Age 29–31: Incipiently Violent Self-Image

I was a divorcé. My wife and I got divorced because she wanted a full-time job and I wanted a wife who stayed home. After we separated, I got into running the streets and chasing women. I just wanted any woman who I could hit on for the night—nothing serious. My people thought I had an untogether social life dogging around after women all the time. But my friends thought I was a party man who always had a lot of fun.

The clique that I was in at work thought I was a heavy rapper and politically hip. I became their representative to the union and management. They considered me a loyal leader because I didn't take any shit from management and I bitched like hell to the union. I had a reputation around the plant as a militant rabble rouser.

People thought that I was a wild, crazy dude but not bad. They knew I would put people in their place. If somebody rubbed my ass good, then I'd ruffle up like a choice rooster, throw a few bad words at them, and act like I was going to step across their chest. But I'd only go so fucking far. I wasn't out to really get down unless I had to. Some people who knew me then said I got into people's asses too quick, and they thought I should lighten up.

Age 29–31: Unsubstantially Violent Period

Age 29: Unsubstantially Violent Acts. I picked up a girl from a bar one night and brought her over to my apartment. We had some food, drank some wine. It was time for romance, but she just backpedaled and announced she was leaving. So I said, "You filled your stomach with food, drank your fill, and now you want to leave, right?" She said, "That's right; I'm leaving." Then I got pissed off at the dirty bitch and slapped her upside the head hard and knocked her down. Then

I opened the door, kicked her in the butt, and told her to get the fuck out. I had a few other similar incidents too, but I never really beat up any of the bitches. [No police.]

Age 30: Unsubstantially Violent Act. I was seeing this woman who was separated from her husband. I picked her up one night from her mother's house, and she asked me where we were going. I told her to a little bar on X street. She got uptight and said, "I didn't get all dressed up for you to take me to some cheap bar." I said, "Well, that's all I can do tonight. I'll take you to a better place some other night." She said, "If that's all you can do, then I'm not about to give you any pussy tonight." I said, "If that's the way you want to be about it, I don't need you." She said, "Well, I didn't need you from the beginning." Then I really got mad and slapped her across the damn face. After I slapped her, she said, "Just take me home," so I did. When she opened the car door and started to get out, I kicked the dirty bitch in the ass. [No police.]

Age 31: Unsubstantially Violent Act. I was at a cabaret when I bumped into a guy and spilled my drink on his date. The guy said, "Hey, man, you spilled your liquor on my woman's dress." I said, "I'm sorry about that." Then he said, "Well, how about you paying to get her dress cleaned?" I said, "Look, it was an accident. I wish I had kept my liquor in my glass." He said, "I don't care what it was. You better give me the money to get her dress cleaned." I had had it with that fucking dude then. I shoved him hard and said, "Get fucked; if you want the money that bad, come on and get it." The other people came over and broke it up. [No police.]

Age 32–38: Nonviolent Self-Image

I have the top job at the plant where I work—a better job than any of the foremen. I'm the full-time union representative for the three hundred men at my shop. I'm their lawyer. I handle all of their problems on the job. They know I have power to move any foremen out of the shop who won't play ball, and they respect me for it. I have a reputation as a bad committee man. Management and union people both see me as a progressive union man who is loyal to the union leadership. Union bosses consider me an up-and-coming committee man who can be groomed for high office. They know I'm a good bargainer and arbitrator and can organize men to follow me. I would say that I have a good future in the union.

My friends at work think that I treat people as individuals and that I'm easy to get along with. They see me as a helpful and warm person who is not uptight. They know that I like to laugh and joke a lot and that I'm a big bullshitter. I can beat most people at it. I can really turn people around with the lines that I lay on them. I enjoy putting bullshit on people because it breaks up the monotony of the day and is a good break from the routine problems on the job.

My second wife thinks that I'm a good husband except that I give too much of my time to my job and I'm occasionally flirty. But she knows that I'm basically a family-oriented man who is 100 percent loyal to her and the kids. I make my family's needs come first even though I like expensive cars and clothes and like to spend money. She knows that I can wear a lot of different caps around the house. I can cook, wash, clean, take care of babies, and be a handyman. My mother and brothers see me as a steady type of individual who makes good money and is reliable and responsible. They think that I know where I'm going and don't get sidetracked. They are real proud of me.

Age 32–38: Negligibly Violent Period

I have had some arguments but not anything close to fights with people during this time.

NOTES

1. In a paper describing findings from a national survey entitled "Middle-Class Violence," Stark and McEvoy (1970) report: "The middle class is not only as likely as others ever to have engaged in physical aggression, but have done so as often. If anything, the middle class is more prone toward physical assault than the poor" (p. 53). This finding may not be so startling considering that the questions this survey used to measure "interpersonal violence" failed to discriminate between unsubstantial and substantial acts of violence. The problems involved in deciding what is a violent crime are discussed briefly by Ferracuti and Newman (1974, pp. 175–77) in their review of "assaultive offenses."

2. This conclusion was drawn from a review of the findings on the ages of violent offenders provided in the following studies: Amir 1971; Bensing and Schroeder 1960; Chappell and Singer 1977; Mulvihill, Tumin, and Curtis 1969; Pokorny 1965a; Voss and Hepburn 1968; and Wolfgang 1958.

9 Conclusions

My study of violent criminality led me to several major and minor conclusions. First, I concluded that individuals will commit violent criminal acts *only after* they form violent interpretations of the situations confronting them. These violent interpretations fall into four types: physically defensive, frustrative, malefic, and frustrative-malefic. Second, I concluded that whether individuals carry out one of these violent interpretations is always *problematic*. It depends on whether they stay in a fixed line of indication or form a restraining or overriding judgment. They will commit violent criminal acts in the first and third cases but not in the second case, which is the most frequent. Because the violent interpretations that individuals form have *variable* outcomes, violent criminal acts are not compulsive actions that, once started, can never be halted.

Third, I concluded that the self-images of individuals who commit violent criminal acts fall into three distinct types: violent, incipiently violent, and nonviolent. Fourth, I concluded that the types of self-images that people hold are always *congruent* with the types of interpretations that they form of the situations in which they commit violent criminal acts. More fully, people who hold nonviolent self-images will commit violent criminal acts only in situations in which they form physically defensive interpretations. Those holding incipiently violent self-images will commit violent criminal acts only in situations in which they form physically defensive or frustrative-malefic interpretations. Finally, those holding violent self-images will commit violent criminal acts in situations in which they form physically defensive or any one of the three offensive interpretations. Thus the type of self-image that people hold is intimately connected to both the *range* and *character* of the situations that they will interpret as calling for violent action, underscoring that their self-images are congruent rather than incongruent with their interpretations.

Finally, I concluded that the careers of violent criminals fall into three basic types: stable, escalating, and de-escalating. In stable careers the types of self-images the violent criminals hold over their lives and the kinds and amounts of violent acts that they commit stay fundamentally the same. In escalating careers the types of self-images the violent criminals hold over their lives become more violent as the kinds of violent acts they commit become more serious and the acts become more frequent. In de-escalating careers the types of self-images that the violent criminals hold over their lives become less violent as the kinds of violent acts they commit become less serious and the acts become more infrequent.

From these five minor conclusions, I drew two major ones. The first one is that people who commit substantially violent acts have different generalized others (see Glaser 1956; Hughes 1962; Shibutani 1955). Those who hold violent self-images have an *unmitigated violent generalized other*—an other providing them with pronounced and categorical *moral* support for acting violently toward other people. Those who hold incipiently violent self-images have a *mitigated violent generalized other*—an other providing them with pronounced, but *limited,* categorical moral support for acting violently toward other people. Finally, those who hold nonviolent self-images have a *nonviolent generalized other*—an other that does not provide them with any pronounced, categorical moral support for acting violently toward other people, *except* in the case of defending themselves or intimates from physical attack.

The second major conclusion that I drew is that the generalized others of violent criminals may change over time. Individuals who have nonviolent generalized others may develop mitigated and then unmitigated violent generalized others, as in the case of escalating violent careers. As this takes place, these individuals will *expand* the range and character of the situations that they will interpret as calling for violence, commit more substantially violent acts, and eventually develop violent self-images. Individuals who have unmitigated violent generalized others may develop mitigated violent and then finally nonviolent generalized others, as in the case of de-escalating violent careers. As this takes place, these individuals will *constrain* the range and character of the situations that they will interpret as calling for violence, commit fewer substantially violent acts, and eventually develop nonviolent self-images.

Thus it is the members of our communities with violent generalized others who are at the heart of our violent crime problem. Not only do they commit the great bulk of serious violent criminal acts, but even as victims they often *precipitate* those that they do not commit. That is, after forming one of the offensive violent interpretations—a frustrative, a malefic, or frustrative-malefic one—they make physically threatening gestures toward people with nonviolent generalized others who then commit violent crimes as a result of forming physically defensive interpretations. In this way people with violent generalized others are responsible for the violent criminal acts committed by people with nonviolent ones.

In short the generalized other plays a crucial part not only in the development of violent criminals but also in such criminals' commission of violent criminal acts. Before a satisfactory explanation of violent crime can ever be developed, however, far more attention needs to be devoted to this seminal idea. More specifically, three questions need to be addressed about the generalized other in future research. First, to what extent, if at all, can the moral support that violent generalized others provide for acting violently toward other people be codified into a specific set of norms or shared rules prescribing violent conduct? Second and more important, regardless of the answer to the first question, what is the nature of the social process promoting the development of such generalized others among certain members of society? Finally, once developed, how can violent generalized others be transformed into nonviolent ones?

Appendix 1   Data on Convicted Violent Offenders

SOURCE AND SELECTION OF PARTICIPANTS

The fifty-eight violent offenders I interviewed for this study came from five institutions in two states. Thirty-five of the offenders were inmates of four different institutions located in a far western state: a large county jail, a women's maximum security prison, and two men's maximum security prisons. The other twenty-three offenders were inmates of a men's maximum security prison located in a midwestern state. All told, forty-eight of the offenders were prison inmates and ten were jail inmates at the time of the interviews.

The violent offenders interviewed were in no sense randomly selected. In fact I made no attempt to select them in any standard way. My only concern was with finding offenders who had committed violent crimes in which they substantially injured someone. Thus the main criterion used in selecting my cases was that the person was serving a sentence for a substantially violent crime. The initial "formal" procedure I used to contact potential subjects for interviews was to ask prison or jail officials if I could examine their records to compile a list of inmates who fulfilled this criterion. This request was usually granted; if it was not, the officials themselves usually compiled such a list for me. One institution that would not allow me to make such a list instead gave me a short list of the inmates who either volunteered in response to some of the treatment staff's announcement of the study in their therapy groups or volunteered in response to an ad placed in the inmates' newspaper.

At any rate, I initially selected the inmates from whatever list I had at my disposal and asked them to participate in the study. Then I tried to start up a "friendship grapevine" by asking the people whom I actually interviewed whether they had any good friends who were serving sentences for violent crimes. If they did, I took down their friends' names and asked them to pass a good word about the study to their friends. Before I asked any of these inmates' friends to participate, I tried to check the official records to ensure that the friends were serving a sentence for a substantially violent crime. At one institution a particularly influential inmate who participated in the study got six or seven of his associates who were serving sentences for substantially violent crimes to participate. I also tried to bump into as many inmates as possible in the prison, so that I could tell them what I was doing and ask them whether they knew anybody who might be interested in participating in the study. If they did, I took down the names of the people mentioned and tried to check the official records to see whether they were serving a sentence for a substantially violent crime. If they were, I then asked them to participate in the study.

This was more or less how I found my subjects at the five institutions where I conducted the study. Although admittedly haphazard, it had an unanticipated benefit. It led me to interview a wide variety of offenders: male and female; young adult and middle-aged; black, white, Oriental, Hispanic, and Native American; upper-, middle-, and lower-class; and urban and rural. The cultural diversity of my subjects prevented me from developing an explanation bound by class, race, gender, or subculture.

Of course, getting violent offenders to participate was a much bigger problem than finding them. I usually saw the inmates privately and explained candidly to them what I was seeking to do. I told them I was a student and I was doing a study about people who committed violent crimes and how they came to commit them. I said that to get this information, I wanted to interview individuals who had committed violent acts and who would speak honestly about themselves and their violent experiences. Then I made it perfectly clear that I did not work for the Department of Corrections, the FBI, the police, and so on; that I would keep all their remarks confidential; and that I would not provide any information on them to the correctional staff, other inmates, or anybody else. After explaining this, I asked whether they had any questions, and they usually did. The most frequent ones were what I was getting out of doing the study; whether I was being paid to do it; if so, by whom; and how their participation was going to help them in the institution. I explained that carrying out a study was part of my graduate degree requirements and that their participation in it would not bear on their future in the institution one way or the other. Another question that often came up was whether I had a tape recorder in the office or in my briefcase. I said no and let them look in my briefcase, in the desk, and around the office.

After I answered all their questions, I emphasized that I wanted to interview only people who would come out with the real facts about themselves and their experiences. Then I asked whether they would be willing to help me out with the study and be interviewed for several hours. Some said they were not. For example, some people who were not interested said, "No way I'm going to run down my crime and things I've done to you; shit, I wouldn't cop out on that to my own mother"; or, "Shit, I'm sorry I can't help you out, but like I'm innocent"; or, "Look, I'll tell you all you want to know about this fucking prison and the parole board or anything else, but I'm appealing my case, and my lawyer told me not to discuss the details with anybody"; or, "I'm just in here for fucking some bitch, not any for-real rape, so I don't righteously have any violent experiences to tell you about." If the person seemed uptight or was adamant, I just said, "Well, thank you for your time," and he left. But if he seemed fairly loose about it, I would say something like "Ninety-nine percent of the people in here say they're innocent, but I'm not interested in whether you should have been found legally guilty or not. I'm just interested in whether you did any violent thing." Occasionally some who originally responded negatively would then agree to be interviewed.

On the other hand, some responded positively right off. For example, they said, "Yeah, sure, I'll help you out; why not? It's not going to hurt me"; or, "Okay, I believe you. I'll do it"; or, "X said it was cool, so I guess I can go along with it"; or, "I'm game. Let's get started"; or, "It would be nice to talk with someone on the outside for change. Go ahead and ask me whatever you want."

The fact that the people I interviewed were selected in a nonrandom and nonstandardized fashion was of no consequence for my study. The conclusions that I sought to draw were not about the statistical distribution of characteristics of violent offenders or offenses; rather, they were primarily about the social psychological processes at work in violent criminal acts. Thus I was concerned only with finding people to interview who had committed substantially violent acts.

CONDUCTING AND VALIDATING THE INTERVIEWS

I conducted all the interviews with the offenders privately and took detailed notes. I checked the notes after each interview or some portion of it was completed and added anything that I didn't have time to write down during the interview. The questions always covered essentially the same set of topics, with two important exceptions. The topics covered were (1) the situation during which the individuals committed the violent criminal act that led to their serving the sentence; (2) the situations in which they almost, but did not, commit violent acts; (3) the self-images they held at the time of their offense; and (4) their violent careers, that is, their past self-images and history of violent experiences. The two exceptions were that I did not ask the individuals at the midwestern institution, where I conducted my first set of interviews, about the near-violent situations that they may have had or about their violent careers.

Further, I did not question every person in exactly the same way on each of these topics. Such a standardized technique would not have been fruitful, because the people whom I interviewed came from a variety of cultural and social backgrounds. I usually tried to adjust the wording of the questions with this in mind. For example, with respect to the first topic I might ask, "X, could you tell me in as much detail as possible how the situation occurred that led to your serving this sentence?" and later I would say, "Now let's go back over this once more, and this time I want you to tell me what, if anything, you were thinking about or feeling and the order that you were thinking or felt it as this situation unfolded." Alternatively I might pose these questions more colloquially, asking, "X, could you run down to me in as much detail as possible what happened in the situation that led to you getting this beef?" Then later I would say, "Now run this down once more, but this time tell me what, if anything, was on your mind and when it crossed your mind as this thing came down." I continued to go over the same topic in this fashion until I felt that I had the facts down pat. Then I would turn to the next topic.

Many times after finishing a topic, the person I was interviewing wanted to engage in conversation unrelated to the study—for example, about sex on campus, sports, music, what I did for entertainment, or women's liberation—so we often took short breaks to discuss such matters before moving on to the next topic. I conducted the interviews with the offenders in such a flexible and informal but systematic manner to help establish and maintain rapport with them. The great degree of rapport that I achieved with the inmates is indicated by the number of first-time criminal admissions that I obtained. During the interviews seven inmates who had previously maintained their innocence admitted to me that they committed the violent crimes for which they had been sentenced.

There was no way for me to validate all the information that the offenders provided during their interviews. The information that I could validate was what they provided on the situation in which they committed the violent criminal act for which they were serving their present sentence and on critical aspects of their violent careers. I validated the former by comparing their account of the situation in which they committed the violent criminal act with that found in the police report. If the offender's description of the "material facts" of the situation differed substantially from the one that the police provided, then I discarded his entire interview. For example, if he reported that the victim was a girlfriend of his whom he went over to see, but the police report indicated that the victim was a stranger whose apartment he forcibly entered, then his interview was thrown out. In most cases it was fairly easy to determine the validity of the offender's account of the situation by this method. Further, this method of validating the offender's account of the situation is more rigorous than it may perhaps appear. It is much more difficult than it may seem to falsify in a detailed and consistent manner the so-called subjective side of a situation, that is, one's perceptions and evaluations, while at the same time not falsifying any of its material, or objective, details. This, of course, is exactly what would have been needed for an offender to falsify deliberately this information to me and not have it detected by the validation procedure that I used.

The offender's account of his violent career could be validated only for the violent crimes for which he was officially charged. I did this by examining each offender's "rap sheet," that is, the list of all crimes for which an individual has been charged, with the date on which he was charged and the disposition of the charges (whether he was arrested or convicted and the sentence that he received). I compared the violent crimes noted on the offender's rap sheet with those that he reported during the interview. If the offender's account of his official violent career did not correspond with that provided by his rap sheet and he could not satisfactorily explain the discrepancy, then I discarded his entire interview.

Further, for many of the offenders I was also able to examine more detailed police reports of past violent crimes for which they were arrested (jail inmates only) or convicted (prison inmates). If any of the offender's accounts of these past violent criminal acts differed substantially in terms of the material facts from the account provided in the police report, then I threw out the interview. The validation methods just described were applied in a strict fashion. I did not keep a count of the number of interviews that were discarded, however. The primary reason for my not keeping a record of this is that I tried not to complete interviews with people who I suspected were deliberately falsifying information to me. Prisons and jails are notorious for their "con" and "bullshit" artists. Whenever I suspected that an inmate was lying to me during an interview, I would use a delaying tactic and then try to check the subject's official records. For example, as soon as I finished covering the particular topic that we were on, I would say, "X, I have an appointment that I forgot about, so we will have to get together later to finish this interview." I usually examined the offender's records beforehand. Then, if he seemed to me beyond reasonable doubt to be falsifying information, I would say something like, "Okay, X, thanks for your help, but I don't need any more cases like yours right now." Incidentally, whenever I had to use either of these tactics, the offender never pursued finishing the interview but just left, so I suspect they knew that I was on to them.

In my judgment the data that were used in the analysis are solid. The descriptions of the offenders whose interviews were used in terms of their offense, sex, and approximate age at the time of the offense are presented in table 1.

Table 1. Description of the Cases

Case No.	Convicted Offense	Sex	Age
1	Criminal homicide	M	mid-20s
2	Criminal homicide	M	mid-20s
3	Criminal homicide	M	late 20s
4	Criminal homicide	M	mid-40s
5	Aggravated assault	M	late 20s
6	Aggravated assault	M	early 20s
7	Criminal homicide and forcible rape	M	midteens
8	Criminal homicide	M	early 20s
9	Forcible rape	M	late 20s
10	Criminal homicide	M	late 20s
11	Criminal homicide	M	midteens
12	Criminal homicide	M	early 30s
13	Criminal homicide	M	mid-30s
14	Forcible rape	M	early 20s
15	Forcible rape	M	late teens
16	Criminal homicide	M	early 30s
17	Criminal homicide and robbery	M	mid-20s

18	Criminal homicide	M	mid-30s
19	Criminal homicide	M	late teens
20	Criminal homicide and robbery	M	mid-20s
21	Aggravated assault and robbery	M	early 20s
22	Criminal homicide	M	early 20s
23	Criminal homicide	M	late 40s
24	Aggravated assault and robbery	M	early 20s
25	Forcible rape and burglary	M	late 20s
26	Aggravated assault	M	early 20s
27	Aggravated assault	M	early 30s
28	Criminal homicide	F	early 40s
29	Aggravated assault	F	early 30s
30	Criminal homicide	F	mid-30s
31	Aggravated assault	F	mid-20s
32	Aggravated assault	F	mid-20s
33	Aggravated assault	M	early 20s
34	Aggravated assault	M	late 20s
35	Aggravated assault	M	early 20s
36	Aggravated assault	F	late teens
37	Criminal homicide	M	mid-20s
38	Criminal homicide	M	late teens
39	Aggravated forcible rape	M	early 20s
40	Forcible rape	M	late teens
41	Aggravated assault and robbery	M	mid-20s
42	Aggravated assault	M	early 20s
43	Forcible rape	M	early 20s
44	Aggravated assault	M	late 20s
45	Criminal homicide	M	early 20s
46	Forcible rape	M	early 20s
47	Aggravated assault	F	mid-20s
48	Aggravated assault	F	early 20s
49	Forcible rape	M	late 20s
50	Aggravated assault	F	late 20s
51	Aggravated assault	F	early 20s
52	Criminal homicide	M	early 20s
53	Forcible rape	F	late teens
54	Forcible rape	M	late teens
55	Criminal homicide	M	late teens
56	Criminal homicide	M	early 30s
57	Criminal homicide	M	mid-30s
58	Criminal homicide	M	late 20s

Appendix 2   Participant Observation of Violent Actors and Acts

The participant observation that I drew on in this research was at the time not done for the purpose of a study. In fact I did this study as the result of my participant observation rather than the other way around. After observing many substantially violent acts and violent actors, I became interested in reading the formal literature on this topic during my first semester as a graduate student. Since I was astonished by the fact that this literature did not correspond with my firsthand observations and experiences, I decided to carry out a study of my own on the problem of violent criminality.

My observations of substantially violent acts and violent actors date as far back as I can remember (beginning about when I was in the third grade) and continued until sometime after I was a college student. Thus it occurred for a period of well over ten years. I should point out, however, that during this time I observed only a couple dozen or so *substantial* violent acts and was well acquainted with less than a half-dozen persons who I knew for a fact had committed and would commit such acts.

Nevertheless I have observed substantially violent acts and actors of a variety of types. The violent people I have known included blacks and whites, as well as old, young, and middle-aged individuals. I have witnessed violent acts ranging from an attempted forcible rape to severe beatings to assaults with deadly weapons. The two most serious violent acts that I observed were a shooting and a stabbing in the eye with a can opener. In the attempted forcible rape the victim was beaten and threatened with a broken bottle. I have also observed on separate occasions a person get smashed in the head with a brick, another hit in the head with a baseball bat, and dishes broken over a person's head. On several other occasions I observed fights where only hands and feet were used but where bones were broken (a cracked rib or broken nose or jaw) and where cuts that required stitches were inflicted. I also saw several severe chokings and many fistfights in which the individuals involved were not substantially physically injured. The perpetrators and victims were in a few instances intimates, in several others neighbors and good acquaintances, and on a couple of occasions complete strangers. Sometimes the police became involved in these incidents, but usually they did not. The incidents were not localized in any specific area. They occurred in fields, in parking lots, in bars, in cars, in a gym downtown (one), on my block, and around schools.

Besides stimulating my initial interest in studying violent crime, my observations and experiences played two crucial roles in the analysis that I carried out here. First, it provided me many valuable hunches with which to build the analytical categories that I used in the study. Second, it provided me an additional source of data against which to check the findings and conclusions of my study. This was particularly crucial since the main source of data used in the analysis came from interviews with convicted violent offenders. For example, I asked myself whether all the individuals whom I had known well and had seen commit substantially violent criminal acts that were not victim precipitated actually held violent or incipiently violent self-images, and if so, whether they had stable, escalating, or de-escalating careers. After this study was initiated, I was also able to talk with a couple of the individuals who I knew for sure had perpetrated or were still perpetrating substantially violent acts and to use their cases in my analysis. These data proved to be especially helpful in the discovery of the de-escalating type of career, since none of the convicted violent offenders had careers of this type. In short, my participant observation of violent actors and acts played an indispensable part in all stages of this study—in its inception, in the collection and analysis of the data, and in the drawing of conclusions.

A SECOND LOOK AT

VIOLENT CRIMINAL ACTS

AND ACTORS

My conviction is that all serious creative work
must be at bottom autobiographical, and that a
man must use the material and experience of
his own life if he is to create anything that
has substantial value.—Thomas Wolfe,
The Story of a Novel

The study described in my book *Violent Criminal Acts and Actors* constitutes the culmination of a larger research project on violent crime that I started more than twenty-five years ago. Thus readers cannot fully appreciate the value of my book until they understand the part that it plays in this larger project. In conducting this research project, I adopted what is now known as an "interpretive" approach (Blumer 1969; Denzin 1989). I wanted not only to contribute to the understanding of violent criminality but also to present a convincing case for taking an interpretive approach in the field of criminology in general, which underlies Herbert Blumer's claim in the foreword to this book that "students in the social sciences in general and in criminology in particular will find the present work to be well worth their study and cogitation." He says that "it opens the door to a much needed form of study in the grand task that confronts criminology."

The auspicious statement that Blumer made more than fifteen years ago was not prophetic. Neither the interpretive approach nor my book has made a big splash in criminology. The interpretive approach is not even recognized by that name. In my cursory survey of recent criminological theory books (Akers 1994; Curran and Renzetti 1994; Lilly, Cullen, and Ball 1995; Vold and Bernard 1986; Williams and McShane 1994), I did not find a single entry with the word *interpretation* or any of its derivatives in their tables of contents or indexes.

My book is hardly mentioned in criminology textbooks, seldom discussed in research articles or monographs, and never noted in government-sponsored reports on violent crime. There are at least two possible reasons for this neglect. First, perhaps the book is simply devoid of insights. The other possible reason, the one to which I obviously subscribe, is that the interpretive approach in general and its application to violent crime in particular constitute a direct challenge, if not an affront, to the criminologists who control what passes and what does not pass for knowledge in their field.[1] Norman Denzin (1989) elaborates on this general point: "Knowledge is intimately related to power.... Those with power determine how knowledge about situations is to be gained. Those who have power determine how knowledge will be defined. Those who have power also define what is not knowledge" (p. 30).

The interpretive approach raises serious questions about assumptions that conventional criminologists take for granted, their accepted procedures, and their real interest in and personal commitment to the problems that they select to study. Thus, to put my research project in the larger intellectual context, I need to discuss briefly the essential differences between the interpretive approach and positivism, the dominant approach in all the social sciences for at least most of this century.

NOTE

1. At least in my case, I am not basing this on mere conjecture. I repeatedly tried to get my work published in mainstream criminological forums, but to no avail. My articles were routinely rejected primarily on the grounds that my methods and procedures were not scientifically sound, which allegedly made my conclusions highly suspect. The editors of these journals repeatedly informed me that the country's "leading experts" on violent crime had drawn this conclusion. In his review Graeme Newman (1980) lodged many of the same criticisms against my book that these reviewers had lodged against my journal articles: "Maybe the failure of the book does do us one service: it points up, albeit in an accentuated fashion, the shallowness of symbolic interactionism and the underlying tautology on which it is built" (289). During those bleak days I took heart from thinking that I must be breaking new ground to provoke such extreme reactions on the part of conventional criminologists. In a similar vein, Sherwood Anderson consoled Thomas Wolfe, who earlier in his career had also experienced trouble getting his work published: "Every man of force and originality has some trouble" (qtd. in Townsend 1987, p. 309). Fortunately I was eventually able to get my work published in highly respected journals that mainstream criminologists did not control.

11 The Conflicting Assumptions of Positivism and Interpretivism

Blumer (1937, 1969, 1981; Athens 1984a, 1993a and b) originally developed the interpretive approach primarily from the ideas of his two former mentors, Robert Park (1938, 1952, 1967) and George Herbert Mead (1932, 1934, 1936; Athens 1994, 1995). Blumer (1956a) eloquently states the raison d'être of this approach: "We can and, I think, must look upon human group life as chiefly a vast interpretative process in which people, singly and collectively, guide themselves by defining the objects, events, and situations which they encounter" (p. 686). The perfectly logical conclusion that he draws from this is that "any scheme designed to analyze human group life in its general character has to fit this process of interpretation" (p. 687). Blumer provides only a generic description of the interpretive approach, however. He describes the approach in terms of its general applicability to the study of all forms of human conduct rather than in terms of its specific applicability to the study of any one particular form: "It is able to cover the full range of the generic forms of human association. It embraces equally well such relationships as cooperation, conflict, domination, exploitation, consensus, disagreement, closely knit identification, and indifferent concern for one another. The participants in each of such relations have the same common task of constructing their acts by interpreting and defining the acts of each other" (1969, p. 67). Thus, according to his description, the interpretive approach can be applied to all aspects of the crime problem (Becker 1973, pp. 177–88), including criminalization, which is the creation and application of the criminal law (Becker 1973, pp. 121–63), and criminality, which is the commission of any act that could potentially make one a criminal.[1]

For present purposes I limit my comparison of the interpretive and positivistic approaches to their application to criminality.[2] At least six significant differences exist between the two approaches. First, they differ with respect to the presumed source of criminal behavior. The positivistic approach assumes that criminal behavior is a product of social, cultural, psychological, or biological factors operating either alone or in conjunction with each other but in either case independently of criminals' interpretations of the situations in which they commit crimes. The interpretive approach assumes that criminals' actions are a product of the individuals' interpretations of these situations, which past experiences always influence in important ways but never completely determine (Athens 1993b, pp. 168–73).

Second, the approaches differ in terms of the attitudes that researchers assume toward their subject matter. To discover the causes of criminal behavior, the positivist assumes the attitude of a detached observer. While studying criminal behavior to discover how criminals interpret the situations that confront them when they commit crimes, the interpretive researcher assumes the attitude of the individuals whose criminal actions are under study.

According to the interpretive approach, researchers who have firsthand knowledge of the criminal activities that they are studying can best assume the attitudes of the individuals who have engaged in those actions (Athens 1984a, 1992; Blumer 1962, 1969; Becker 1966; Cooley 1926; Denzin 1989). "Unlike the positivists, who separate themselves from the worlds they study," Denzin (1989) explains, "the interpretivists participate in the social world so as to understand and express more effectively its emergent properties and features" (p. 25). Participation in the social worlds that one studies is an indispensable condition for gaining what Cuthbertson and Johnson (1992) aptly call "exquisite emotional sensitivity," which is necessary, although by no means sufficient, for understanding the actors who comprise those worlds. The requirement that criminologists must either have been exposed to the criminal's world or at least be willing to enter it is especially repugnant to positivists, who prefer not to cavort with common street criminals but to study them from a safe distance instead (Clinard 1966, pp. 404–5). I believe that this is the biggest source of the disdain that positivists frequently express for the interpretive approach, since their backgrounds usually prepare them to deal with white-collar criminals more effectively than with common street criminals.

A third major difference between positivistic and interpretive approaches relates to the kind of concepts that should be used in studying criminal behavior. According to positivistic approaches, researchers should use "definitive" concepts, or what are often called "operational definitions," because they pave the way for subsequent complex statistical analyses. Definitive concepts specify the exact attributes of the criminals and their behavior to be examined before their actual study. According to the interpretive approach, however, the researcher should use what Blumer (1954, pp. 7–8) labels "sensitizing" concepts, which only suggest the general outline of the problem to be examined before it is actually studied in detail. Furthermore the interpretive approach encourages researchers to delay precisely specifying the attributes of the criminality under examination until after they have studied it in considerable depth. Whereas positivists begin their studies with definitive concepts, the interpretivists, who recognize that true definitive concepts are impossible in the social sciences, end their studies only with more definitive sensitizing concepts (Athens 1984a, pp. 243–44; Park 1952, p. 173). "Among The Scientists [Positivists], the most frequent type is The Higher Statistician, who breaks down truth and falsity into such fine particles that we cannot tell the difference between them," Mills (1963, p. 569) observes. Thus the interpretive approach supports a much more flexible and open-ended inquiry into criminality than the positivistic approach does (Athens 1984a; Blumer 1954, 1969, pp. 21–60).

Fourth, the two approaches use different models of causation in their research. The positivistic approach advocates a mechanical model of causation that assumes that certain antecedent factors operating under certain specified conditions produce criminal behavior. Thus, according to positivists, the criminologist's job is to identify these specific antecedent factors and the specific conditions under which the factors operate. The interpretive approach advocates a processual model of causation. This model assumes that criminal conduct is always produced by certain developmental processes whose earlier stages do not automatically determine their later ones. Thus, according to interpretivists, the criminologist's job is to identify the processes whereby interpretations of situations favorable to taking criminal actions emerge, sustain themselves, change, and—one hopes— disappear (Athens 1984a, pp. 244–45, 1993b, pp. 168–73; Lindesmith 1981).

Fifth, the positivistic and interpretive approaches differ with respect to their views of the criminal. In the positivistic approach the criminals are treated as "passive agents" whose criminal acts are products solely of causal factors that may be internal, external, or both (Blumer 1969, pp. 14–15). A human being's decision to engage in crime is thereby effectively relegated to the status of an epiphenomenon. Although human beings may decide to commit crimes, the decisions that they make are caused by factors to which they are oblivious. Since the decision to commit a crime results from causal factors that lie outside the criminals' conscious control, they play no part in their criminality (Blumer 1969, pp. 14–15).

Conversely the interpretivists treat criminals as "actors" who must assemble their actions as best as they can based on their past experiences in handling situations similar to the one at hand (Mead 1934, pp. 214–15; Thomas 1967, pp. 41–42). Of course situations may always contain novel aspects and contingencies for which our past experiences never completely prepare us. Thus our past experiences can never completely determine our present decisions, although they definitely affect the choices that we consider when adopting a course of action. Since human beings are normally aware of at least some of the contingencies that confront them in any situation, they can always exercise some degree of control over their conduct. At bare minimum they can decide whether to pursue or avoid a particular course of action. A human being's decision to commit a criminal act is thereby elevated from the status of epiphenomenon to that of real decision. Human beings thus always play a part, however minuscule, in their becoming criminals. Nevertheless, unless the decision to engage in crime is treated with utmost seriousness, the nature and magnitude of the part played by the individual in becoming a criminal are lost from sight, as they are for the positivist.

Finally, the two approaches differ with respect to their preferred modes of intellectual production. The positivists usually prefer the corporate system of production, where members of a large research team work in an organizational hierarchy with a director at the top, senior researchers at the second-to-highest level, junior researchers at the step below, and research assistants at the bottom. Instead of independent thought, "groupthink" is encouraged, but the thoughts expressed must remain within acceptable limits that the director and senior staff unofficially set but, should the need arise, officially enforce.

The positivists often tailor the problems selected for study and the methods chosen for studying these problems to fit the special needs of government granting agencies. In reaction to this notorious practice on their part, almost thirty years ago Blumer (1967) voiced the still-heretical opinion that

the primary source of the corrupting influence is the lure that agency-determined research casts in the form of sizable allotments of

funds for research and in the form of the prestige that is seemly yielded by connection with high level government work. . . . Under the
pressure to have funds, many are ready to bend their research interests and efforts in the directions laid down by available funds. . . . To
be engaged in a research undertaking of large magnitude, to have a
large amount of money for its execution, and to command the assistance of a sizable corps of research workers on the project have become, I think unfortunately, a ponderable standard of successful
achievement in social science research today. (pp. 167–68)

In sharp contrast, interpretivists prefer to work alone or in pairs on a
problem that they have independently carved out from their personal experiences together with their critical reading of the literature on the topic.
Whereas the interpretivists view what they do as an intellectual craft, the
positivists see their work as "scientific research." Mills (1963) quips,
"Among them, I am sure, are those who would love to wear white coats
with an IBM symbol of some sort on the breast pocket" (p. 569). By drawing on their bank of personal experiences, the interpretivists can gain some
inkling as to whether something is askew in the accepted explanations of
crime that are promulgated in the formal criminological literature. "Our
science has grasped," as Mead (1936) perceptively noted over fifty years
ago, "that precious peculiarity of the scientist that enables him to get hold
of the problem whose solution gives a new heaven and new earth" (p. 413).
Thus personal experience is transformed from a potential source of bias
whose use the positivists eschew to a rich and indispensable resource that
the interpretivists can draw from with all their hearts' desire. "Everything
in a work of art," Wolfe (1936) contends, "is changed and transfigured by
the personality of the artist" (p. 22). Wolfe's statement is as true for criminology as it is for literature. The interpretivists' interest in the problems
that they select for study emanate first and foremost from their personal
experiences rather from their desire to garnish government funding and
secure academic power, which is typically the case with positivists, since
more often than not the interpretivists must fund their studies from their
own pockets.[3]

NOTES

1. See, for example, Becker 1953; Denzin 1984, 1985, 1986, 1987; Douglas
1967; Katz 1988; Lindesmith 1968; and Thomas 1967.

2. It is worthwhile to point out that labeling theory applies features of the interpretive approach to the crime problem; its application of this approach is faulty, however. The theory downplays the distribution of various kinds of criminals in the community, while it plays up the distribution of various kinds of social control agents, such as police and probation officers (see, for example, Erickson 1966, pp. 24–26). While social control agents' actions are emphasized, the criminals' actions are minimized (Athens 1992, pp. 86–89). This emphasis not only dramatizes the formal actions taken by social control agents that affect a person's official status as a "criminal," such as arrest and conviction, but also minimizes the informal actions taken by his family, close friends, and neighbors that affect his self-conception and, more important, his phantom community (Finestone 1976, pp. 206–14). Finally, while the criminal label that social control agents attach to the person is accentuated, his ultimate acceptance or rejection of that label is trivialized (Athens 1992, pp. 72–75; Finestone 1976, pp. 214–15). Thus, because the interpretive approach cannot be reduced to labeling theory, the comparison between positivism and interpretivism is more relevant than that between positivism and labeling theory.

3. Although my critique of positivism will undoubtedly strike conventional criminologists as unduly harsh, it is well deserved. Since criminology's development in America, positivists have maintained a stranglehold over resources available in this field. Unfortunately intellectual return from their research simply does not justify their continued monopolization of our scarce resources.

12 The Origin of My Interest in Violent Crime

In his famous essay "On Intellectual Craftmanship," Mills (1959) advises students that "the most admirable thinkers within the scholarly community you have chosen to join do not split their work from their lives. They seem to take both too seriously to allow such disassociation" (p. 195). Mills importantly adds that "they want to use each for the enrichment of the other" (p. 195). I take Mills's dictum on intellectual craftsmanship seriously. In fact, it provided the original inspiration for my research project on violent crime. As I say in appendix 2 to part 1:

> The participant observation that I drew on in this research was at the time not done for the purpose of a study. In fact I did this study as a result of my participant observation rather than the other way around. After observing many substantially violent acts and violent actors, I became interested in reading the formal literature on this topic during my first semester as a graduate student. Since I was astonished by the fact that this literature did not correspond with my firsthand observations and experiences, I decided to carry out a study of my own on the problem of violent criminality.

In the same appendix I describe my participant observation of violent criminal acts and actors this way:

> My observations of substantially violent acts and experiences with violent actors date as far back as I can remember. . . . During this time I observed only a couple of dozen or so *substantially* violent acts!çnd was well acquainted with less than a half-dozen persons who I knew for a fact had committed and would commit such acts.

Nevertheless I have observed substantially violent acts and actors of a variety of types. The violent people I have known included black and whites, as well as old, young, and middle-aged individuals. I have witnessed violent acts ranging from an attempted forcible rape to severe beatings to assaults with deadly weapons. The two most serious violent acts that I observed were a shooting and a stabbing in the eyes with a can opener.

In his review of my book, cultural anthropologist Henry Lundsgaarde (1981) raised questions that cast aspersions on my moral character: "What was the exact role of the author as 'participant observer' in these situations? Did he call the police, offer assistance to the victims, flee the scene, or simply observe?" (p. 16). Since Professor Lundsgaarde has raised questions about matters that professional colleagues and college administrators have been wondering about for a long time, let me take this opportunity to answer them, at least for the most serious violent incidents in which I was "implicated."

In the case of the shooting, I played the role of an innocent bystander. I was at a bar that my father operated. While I was playing a pinball machine, a former patron whom my father had told never to enter the bar again suddenly walked through the door. When my father ordered him to leave, he became irate and picked up a bottle from the counter. When he raised the bottle over his head, my father drew his pistol from under the counter. As the man threw the bottle, my father fired his gun several times. The bottle missed my father, but the man was struck once in the torso. My father was later convicted of illegal possession of a firearm. In the attempted forcible rape, where the victim was beaten and threatened with a bottle, I played the role of the good Samaritan. I demanded that the intoxicated attacker stop assaulting the victim. He then threatened me with the bottle. While chasing me around his parked car with the bottle, he finally stumbled to the ground and, luckily for me, passed out. I was a high school student at the time, and the attack took place at a "lover's lane"–type setting. I drove the woman, who was very shaken and whose clothes were badly torn, to my date's home. Since I never received a summons to testify in court, I presume that the attacker was never prosecuted.

When I saw a man get stabbed in the eyes with the can opener, I played the role of an innocent bystander. As a teenager I sometimes worked as an attendant at a parking lot across the street from a stadium. After a game one night, two groups of intoxicated men and women engaged in an ugly argument as they returned to their cars. While one group was getting beer from a cooler in their car's trunk, a member of the second group ran over to them, cursing. Suddenly a member from the first group repeatedly gouged the eyes of the man from the other group with a can opener. I was so terrified by the incident that I can still recall the victim putting his hands to his face and screaming, "Oh shit, one of those dirty SOBs has gouged out my eyes. Help me, help me; I can't see, I can't see, I am blind." While he screamed in terror, the police arrived at the scene.

I also witnessed the brutal murder of a woman, which I did not mention in my book's appendix. During this incident I also played the role of an innocent bystander. I was an adolescent sitting in a booth in the bar that my father operated, and a man stabbed a woman to death outside. My booth was adjacent to a window from which I could see the attack; the woman was slain only a few feet from the large plate-glass window. As the man chased her, the woman ran into a doorway for protection. As she held onto the inside handle of the storm door and screamed for someone to open the main door, her assailant smashed the storm door's glass pane and repeatedly stabbed her through the shattered glass with a knife. While stabbing the woman, the assailant cut his arm badly below the elbow with the glass shards on the storm door. Immediately after the attack, he ran into the bar, spurting blood all over, brandishing his knife, and demanding that my father tie a tourniquet around his arm. After my father did as the man ordered, the man ran out of the bar without noticing me trembling in the booth next to the window. The police and an ambulance arrived on the scene while I frantically explained to my father what the man had done to the woman who was slumped down and bleeding profusely in the doorway outside.

Finally, I was a victim of violent crime as a young child. While I was walking home from elementary school, three teenage boys began calling me "short legs" and taunting me relentlessly about my small stature. After I thought they had walked a safe distance away from me, I made the mistake of yelling back at them. They suddenly began running after me. I cut across a vacant lot in a vain attempt to escape them. Once in the lot, they began throwing rocks and bottles at me as I ran. I was able to avoid getting hit until I tripped on a empty tin can. Just as I got back on my feet, one of the boys ran up to me and bashed me in the head with a brick. As I wobbled backward and put my hands to my head, I saw stars, black splotches, and blood pouring all over my hands and down my shirt. Then I got dizzy and collapsed. I woke up in the hospital, thanks to the kind intervention of a woman who had seen me lying on the ground.

Why was I not more open before about the details of the violent acts that

I had witnessed, my relationship to the violent criminals that I had known, and the role that I had played as an observer? I feared the impact that such disclosures might have on the academic career to which I aspired. In his essay "The Social Role of the Intellectual," Mills (1963) poignantly captures the trepidation that I felt:

> Although, in general, the larger universities are still the freest of places in which to work, the trends which limit the independence of the scholar are not absent there. . . . Yet the deepest problem of freedom for teachers is not the occasional ousting of a professor, but a vague general fear—sometimes politely known as "discretion," "good taste," or "balanced judgement." It is a fear which leads to self intimidation and finally becomes so habitual that the scholar is unaware of it. The real restraints are not so much external prohibitions as control of the insurgent by the agreements of academic gentlemen. (pp. 296–97)

Of course Mills's concern dealt with the plight of radical scholars. They are now in far less dire straits than they were when Mills voiced this legitimate concern more than fifty years ago (Jacoby 1987, pp. 140–90). Today there are more radical than interpretive criminologists entrenched in universities, although positivists easily outnumber either group. Evidently the university establishment considers those who demand that firsthand knowledge be taught inside the university more subversive than those who call for a revolution outside the university to bring about a crime-free world sometime in the distant future.

In my particular case, I was afraid to be found guilty by association and treated as riffraff, a rogue, or even worse, a criminal rather than a criminologist, and thereby deemed unfit for university service even though I have never been arrested or convicted for any crimes other than minor traffic violations. My fears were well founded. College administrators have asked me, "Is there anything about your past that we should know about?" Painfully naive colleagues from cloistered worlds have repeatedly inquired whether I have ever committed any violent crimes. I have overheard others who have scanned my books whisper their suspicions about my past life to one another and voice concerns about my presence in their midst.

After giving oral presentations about my research during job interviews, professors have gasped, "He may be a criminologist, but then again, he may also be a violent criminal." At American Society of Criminology meetings, I have made the faux pas of asking whether a panelist had any firsthand knowledge about violent crime, as well as referring to my own firsthand experience, both of which never fail to draw an indignant reaction. I agree with Mills (1959) that social scientists should not split their work from their lives, which he laments "is the prevailing condition among men in general, deriving . . . from the hollowness of the work which men in general now do" (pp. 195–96). In addition splitting your work from your personal life can make you guilty of professional voyeurism and crass opportunism, two accepted and rampant practices among academic criminologists (Clinard 1966, pp. 404–7). Nevertheless, in the light of my past experiences, I strongly advise criminologists not to advertise that their past lives sparked their interest in their present work, because it can permanently taint their professional reputations as criminologists, even if they were never "criminals" themselves. This says more about universities, which paradoxically prefer to hire professors who have no firsthand experience related to the subjects they teach, than it does about the truth of Mills's dictum.

13 The Preliminary Phase: The Self and the Violent Criminal Act

Violent Criminal Acts and Actors represents the culmination of my first research project on the problem of violent criminal behavior. Six years before its publication, I had published the preliminary phase in a little-known article with this chapter's subtitle as its title. Since the book was a direct outgrowth of this earlier research, I briefly outline that research here. The first phase of my research began with a small exploratory study conducted in 1971–72 that aimed to examine violent criminal behavior from an interpretive point of view. When I first began my studies on criminal violence, there were virtually no published studies that had been conducted from an approach that was even remotely similar to an interpretive one. The only possible exception of which I am aware is Hans Toch's study *Violent Men,* which was published in 1969.

In Toch's study repetitively violent male offenders described several past "violent incidents" in which they had been involved to other inmates or parolees who were specially trained to play the role of interviewers. Toch and the interviewers examined the accounts of these incidents to uncover the common underlying motives that different men repeatedly expressed for their violent actions. Toch (1969) explains the rationale behind this: "We should be able to reconstruct a man from a sample of his violent acts. Why? Because we expect the situations that provoke a man to be stamped out of a common psychological mold. We expect his aggressive acts to be guided and shaped by needs they subserve. . . . We expect them to express a man's 'personality,' in the technical sense of the word" (p. 133).

Based on the examinations of these accounts, Toch concluded that violent men have one of two basic personality types, each encompassing distinct subtypes. In the first type, which may called the "inadequate personality," violence is used to either protect or enhance one's self-worth (Toch 1969, p. 135). There are five subtypes of inadequate personalities: "rep defender," "norm enforcer," "self-image compensator," "self defender," and "pressure remover." In the second type, which may be labeled the "warped personality," violence is an expression of extreme egocentricity, utilitarianism, or both (136). There are only four subtypes of these warped personalities: "bully," "exploiter," "self indulger," and "catharter."

Although the interview process by which Toch gathered his data makes it appear at first glance that his study is based on an interpretive approach, a closer examination leads to a distinctly different conclusion. In the interpretive approach the actor's interpretation of a situation is always considered to be important in its own right and is never seen as completely predetermined by his personality, because what is going on in the immediate operating situation must be always taken into account. Toch constructed a typology of violent persons but not of interpretations of violent situations. Thus the only part that the interpretations of violent situations or "incidents" played in Toch's analysis was to provide him with the information necessary to construct a typology of violent men based exclusively on their personalities. By constructing his typology on that old, dubious assumption, Toch contradicted a fundamental tenet of the interpretive approach (Blumer 1969, pp. 3–4). Consequently his study is ultimately based on the same worn-out causal logic that one sees in conventional personality studies that point to a person's psychological makeup as the antecedent factor responsible for violent behavior (see my discussion in chap. 2). It should be noted that Toch's study took an important step in the right direction, since he did at least try to use violent men's own interpretations of the situations in which they became violent, although he did so incorrectly (Athens 1986, pp. 370–71).

Because no other studies of criminal violence based on an interpretive approach had been conducted at that time, I decided to conduct a small exploratory study. In this study I examined both the interpretations of the situations that offenders formed when they committed substantially violent criminal acts and the self-conceptions that they held at the approximate time in their lives when they committed these acts (Athens 1974). The data for this study were collected primarily through in-depth interviews with violent offenders. During the interviews I asked the violent offenders how they thought their significant others saw them, how they evaluated their significant others' views of them, and what they thought and felt, if anything, when they committed their violent criminal acts.

In his book *Violent Men* Toch (1969, pp. 8–18) reports training inmates and ex-inmates to serve as interviewers instead of conducting the interviews himself. The problem with using specially trained inmates as interviewers, however, is that other inmates are often reluctant to discuss their past criminal behavior too deeply or frankly with each other because they know that, sooner or later, potentially damaging information could make its way through the "prison pipeline." They thus quite understandably tend to give and accept the hackneyed excuses for their offenses, which I believe accounts for the superficial accounts of violent incidents that fill the pages of Toch's often-cited book. In any event, the most important thing for an interviewer to keep in mind is that the subjects must affirm rather than transform the meaning of their violent interpretations or experiences. In his lectures on advanced social psychology, Blumer (Athens 1993b) underscored the importance of this point: "What a scientist should do is discern, as best he can, how the subjects, whose behavior he seeks to explain, define the object that they act toward. In doing this, the scientist must not, however, let his interaction with the subject transform the meaning of the object that the subject holds. This does not necessarily have to occur, for the meanings of objects may undergo affirmation as well as transformation in the interaction between the subject and the scholar" (p. 183).

Based on my analysis of the data that I gathered from my interviews, I drew the following three conclusions. (1) The interpretations of situations that violent offenders form when they commit substantially violent acts fall into four types: "physically defensive," "frustrative," "malefic," and "frustrative-malefic." (2) The violent offenders exhibited two basic types of self-conceptions: "violent" and "nonviolent." (3) A relationship exists between the offenders' self-conceptions and their interpretations of the conflictive situations in which they committed their violent criminal acts, which provided the basis for my formulating the following proposition:

> Actors who hold nonviolent self images commit violent criminal acts in those situations in which they form physically defensive interpretations. Those holding violent self images, on the other hand, commit violent criminal acts in situations in which they form malefic, frustrative, and frustrative-malefic interpretations, as well as physically defensive interpretations. In short, actors with nonviolent self images respond violently on the basis of physically defensive interpretations whereas those with violent self images do so on the basis of any of the four interpretations here posited. (Athens 1974, p. 107)

THE LARGER THEORETICAL IMPLICATIONS

My article has two important theoretical implications, which I unfortunately did not recognize sufficiently at the time. The first implication is that violent criminal acts are products of people's interpretations of conflictive situations, and in constructing these interpretations, individuals' emotions are every bit as important as their thoughts. In fact thinking about their raw feelings creates their emotions (Athens 1994, p. 525; Denzin 1986). In physically defensive interpretations of conflictive situations, the chief emotion created from the individuals' cogitations is fear; in pure frustrative interpretations it is anger; in pure malefic interpretations it is hate; and in frustrative-malefic interpretations it is anger, which subsequently becomes hatred (Athens 1986, pp. 375–80). Thus violent criminal acts are interpretively constructed (Denzin 1985, 1986, pp. 161–200; Katz 1988, pp. 12–51, 164–94, 274–309), and they embody both thoughts and emotions.

In contrast the positivists do not view the violent criminal act as an interpretive construction. For example, Edwin Megargee (1982) describes these acts as products of an "internal" and thereby unconscious "algebra":

> Most human behavior, including violent behavior, is performed fairly automatically. . . . When we analyze a single response we become aware that each act results from the interaction of many factors and comprises dozens of often unconscious choices.
>
> In most situations, you can make any one of a number of different responses. If you are threatened, you can fight, run away. . . .
>
> How do you choose? Typically, you select the response that appears to offer the maximum satisfactions and the minimum dissatisfactions. . . . By means of this internal algebra, which occurs so rapidly you are often unaware of it, you calculate the net strength of each possible response, compare it with all other responses, and select the strongest. (pp. 124–25)

With the help of an algebraic expression complete with variables, operation symbols, and subscripts, Megargee specifies more precisely the "internal algebra" by which a particular violent criminal act j becomes committed against target t–1:

$$(A_{j \cdot t-1}) + (H) + (S_a) > (I_{j \cdot t-1}) + (S_i).$$

Megargee defines the various terms in this equation and explains their operation as follows: "The strength of the instigation for this behavior $(A_{j \cdot t-1})$

plus habit strength (H), as well as any facilitating stimuli in the environment (S_a) must exceed the total strength of internal inhibitions against the commission of this act against this target ($I_{j_t t-1}$)—as well as any environmental stimuli which may impede the expression of this behavior (S_i)" (pp. 126–27). Now we must ask whether the algebraic principles of this violence equation are isomorphic with the principles that govern the violent criminal actions to which Megargee applies it. If the two are not in sync, then his formulation of this equation, no matter how impressive it looks, amounts to a meaningless mathematical exercise (Athens 1984b, pp. 263–65; Blumer 1940, pp. 710–11; Cicourel 1964, pp. 7–38; Gould 1983, pp. 239–72).

If violent criminal acts are the product solely of an internal algebra, then violent criminals do not decide to commit violent crimes; rather, this internal algebra automatically decides for them. According to this explanation, since the typical violent criminal plays the part only of a passive agent or neutral medium in his violent criminal behavior, he could not be found guilty of a violent crime where the determination of guilt requires proof of intent to inflict great bodily harm or death—which of course contradicts both common sense and criminal law.

The second implication of my study is that not only are violent criminal acts a product of an interpretive process, but violent criminals differ from one another in important respects. The observation that not all violent criminals are the same is by no means a revelation on my part. Toch (1969), Megargee (1966, 1973), Banay (1952), and Bjerre (1927) already established this. The new point that my study implies, however, is that not all violent criminals are equally violent (Athens 1986, p. 373). Criminologists must not only distinguish the different types of violent criminals but also place the offenders on qualitatively distinct points of the violence continuum (Athens 1986, pp. 375–80).

UNANSWERED QUESTIONS

Although my study shed new light on previously unstudied aspects of violent criminality, it left several significant questions about these matters unanswered. First, I did not address why people's self-images are linked to their violent interpretations of conflictive situations. I stated a second unanswered question in my study's conclusion: "It should be made explicit that it is not here implied that every time one of the interpretations posited is formed, violence results, but rather, that given that a serious violent crime has occurred, one of these interpretations was necessarily at play.

What remains to be done in future research is to discern when these interpretations lead to violence and when they do not" (Athens 1974, p. 110).

A final troubling question that my study raised but could not answer was whether my findings about the self-conceptions of violent offenders and their interpretations of conflictive situations would hold for a more diverse group of violent criminals, including women. Studies of violent criminals' psychological makeups are notorious for excluding women on the grounds that their relatively infrequent participation in violent crimes makes their study unnecessary; in fact the opposite is true. Since women turn to violence less often than men, it becomes more imperative to study them to determine whether their violent criminal acts represent a genuine anomaly that differs in explanation from that of men's violent crimes.

14 The Principal Phase, I: Violent Criminal Acts and Actors

The main phase of my research project consisted of another, larger study that was conducted to answer the questions left by the preceding one, as well as the further important question of the nature of violent criminals' careers. Although I used the same basic approach and techniques in both studies, there are two significant differences. The first major difference between the two studies was that in the later study I interviewed both male and female offenders, as well as people who had committed serious violent crimes but had managed to escape imprisonment (see appendixes 1 and 2).

Of course, it would have been preferable not to have used any incarcerated violent criminals as subjects for either study. According to standard positivistic reasoning, studies based on incarcerated offenders produce faulty conclusions because inmates represent a select group of criminals. After reading Edwin Sutherland's (1973) enlightening essay "The Prison as a Criminological Laboratory," however, I became convinced that the use of inmates as the principal subjects in a study is warranted where the study's goal is to identify generic processes rather than to draw statistical conclusions about the lives of dangerous criminals:

> There are two difficulties confronting the study of criminals in prison. . . . First, prisoners are a selected group of criminals. Not all criminals are committed to prison and those who are committed are likely to differ from those outside prison. . . . Consequently, unless data regarding prisoners are corrected, they cannot be used statistically as a means of drawing!èonclusions regarding criminals. It is possible, nevertheless, to make studies of prisoners which will throw light on the processes by which criminality develops.

A second difficulty in the use of the prison as a "laboratory" is that the prisoner is not in his "natural habitat." It has been asserted that a criminal can no more be understood in prison than a lion can be understood in a cage. . . . Access to the criminal who is not in confinement is extremely difficult. The basic studies need to be made at a point where the criminal is accessible, and these may be supplemented by occasional analyses of those who are less easily accessible. Aside from that, this argument seems to be relatively unimportant. The habitat which is significant is found in the interpretations of the criminal, and he carries his interpretations with him. (Sutherland 1973, pp. 249–50)

Sutherland concluded his incisive argument by stating: "In spite of the limitations, the prison has decided advantages as a place in which to study the criminal. This is especially true in regard to the older, more difficult, and more dangerous criminals" (250).

Although I strongly agree with the overall thrust of his argument, I believe that he may have unintentionally given the false impression that it is safe and easy to study incarcerated violent criminals. This may be true relatively speaking, but it was definitely not true in the absolute sense when I conducted my research. While interviewing violent offenders, I was physically assaulted on three separate occasions. Because discussing these incidents would divert too much from my main purpose, I will limit my discussion to the most mind-boggling incident, which occurred with the collusion of some correctional staff members.

I was interviewing inmates at a correctional institution near a university where there was considerable student unrest. Many of the correctional facility's staff members had a strong dislike for anyone connected in any way with the university. They made their dislike apparent to me by frequently making snide comments about the university and its students in my presence and by creating lengthy delays in my passage through control gates located throughout the institution. One time while I waited for an inmate to come into the cell that I was using as an interview room, a correctional officer said, "Hey, aren't you that guy from the university who is studying violent criminals?" After I said that I was, he said, "There's a guy here named X that you got to interview."

Surprised that I had not come across the inmate's name when I combed the institution's files, I asked, "Who? What's he done?"

"Hell, he's done it all—rape, murder, robbery, mayhem—you name it," the officer said.

My suspicion was aroused because I could not believe that I had missed this inmate's name in the records. "Well, thanks for letting me know about him. I'll check out his case file and set up an interview with him later," I said.

With an incredulous look on his face, the officer said, "Later? You can't interview this guy later. We are shipping him out of here first thing tomorrow morning. Look, it's either now or never." Before I could say another word, he added, "Don't worry about it; I'll cancel your next interview and bring him instead."

As I sat in the doorway of the empty cell, I began wondering why a correctional officer whom I had never seen before would offer to help me. Then I noticed that the music coming through the facility's sound system suddenly grew much louder. A strange, vague foreboding came over me. While waiting for my next interviewee, I walked down the cell block to the cell of an inmate with whom I had often talked and to whom I had given cigarettes. "Charles," I said, "what's going on? Do you know an inmate named X? What's with the music? I can barely hear myself think."

"Lonnie, you're being set up," Charles said. "Nobody gonna help you, Lonnie. You got to hold up your own pants now. You best be ready to fight when they bring that motherfucker down to your cell. He ain't no for-real bad dude; he just a shaker and a faker." Before I could ask Charles whether he was putting me on about "holding my own pants up" and being ready to fight, the correctional officer appeared with the inmate in tow.

"I got inmate X for you," he said. "Are you ready to interview him?"

"No, I would rather interview inmate Y, who I had originally planned to see," I replied.

"Look, I got him here now, and the shift is about to change, so there is no way that I'm taking him back to his cell block now and getting Y, so you might as well interview him," the officer said.

When we walked into the interview cell, the officer locked the door, which had never been done before. "Open the cell door! Leave it open!" I shouted.

He laughed. "Sorry, regulations," he said.

Locked in that small cell, which was no bigger than an elevator, I felt claustrophobia set in immediately.

As I sat down, inmate X stared coldly at me from the other side of the desk. I asked him what his rap was.

"Booty robbing," he said.

Starting to become fearful, I replied, "Booty robbing?"

"That's right, college boy, booty robbing. Do you know what that is?"

"I think I do," I said. Trying desperately to stall for time to collect my thoughts, I started firing off questions: "How long you been doing it?"

"As long as I can remember," he replied.

"How often did you do it?" I asked.

"As often as I can. I love taking booty—young, old, man, or woman, it don't make a shit to me." Then, with a dour expression on his face and no trace of humor in his voice, he asked me, "Tell me something, college boy: has anybody ever had your booty?"

My fear grew as he stared into my eyes while waiting for my reply. I now knew that Charles had not been joking. It was true—the guards had set me up. Since they would not come to my aid, there was no use screaming for their help. I was on my own. I told myself that I had no choice but to fight with all the might and fury I had in me. Bracing myself for action, I quickly scanned the distance between us, the walls of the cell, and the top of the desk, which barely fit into the tiny cell.

He broke the long silence, saying, "You know, college boy, there two ways you can get your booty taken, the easy or the hard way. It don't make no difference to me, 'cause I like either way. So the only real question is which fucking way do you want me to take it, the hard or easy?"

When he reached over the desk and grabbed me around my shirt collar, I screamed, "The hard way, the hard, hard!" I grabbed the bottom of the top desk drawer and began standing up while tilting the desk toward him. The edge of the desktop him hit above the knees, and then I pushed the desk with all my strength until it rolled completely over him, knocking him to the floor. As he laid flat on his back with the desk firmly planted across his torso and his breath knocked out, I jumped on top of the now upside-down desk, putting my full body weight on it. I had managed to pin him on the floor of the small cell. As he laid there helpless, unable to move his torso, arms, or legs in any direction, I yelled for the correctional officers, who to my surprise appeared quickly despite the blare of the music. After the two officers appeared, one of whom had originally arranged the interview with this inmate, the volume of the music suddenly dropped. They offered to write up the inmate, but I told them that I preferred to forget about the incident for the time being. They assured me that nothing like that would ever happen to me again in their institution and that in the future I could count on their complete cooperation with my study.

The fate that I had narrowly escaped that day haunted me as I continued my interviews at this and other institutions. The stark realization that some correctional officers represented as much of a threat to me as some inmates was unnerving. Based on my past experience interviewing violent offenders, I was prepared for an inmate occasionally "going off" on me, but I did not expect correctional officers to sic inmates on me. Feeling extremely vulnerable, I questioned the wisdom of continuing the study.

Information about people travels remarkably fast among both the staff and inmates across different correctional institutions. My declining to file a complaint against this inmate greatly enhanced other inmates' respect for me, which in turn increased their willingness to participate in my study, not only at this institution, but at others in the state as well. On the other hand, correctional administrators became more distrustful of me, which at some institutions led them to search me thoroughly every time I passed through their gates (see Johnson 1975, pp. 50–144).

The other important difference between my two studies is that the scope of the interviews for the second one was much broader. In my second study I collected not only the same information as I did in my first study but also information on two new matters: the subjects' violent careers and the situations in which they almost committed substantially violent criminal acts but did not. Thus during the interviews for my second study, I also asked the subjects about the past violent acts they committed over their entire lives, their past self-conceptions, and their thoughts and feelings during "near-violent situations," those when they almost committed violent criminal acts.

This study yielded several important findings. First, both studies uncovered the same four types of interpretations of situations that people form when committing substantially violent acts (Athens 1977). In the later study, however, I was also able to ascertain when these interpretations lead people to commit substantially violent criminal acts and when they do not. I did this by comparing interpretations of situations in which people almost committed substantially violent criminal acts with interpretations of situations in which they actually committed such acts (chap. 5).

I found that whether people carry out one of these four interpretations depends on whether they stay in a "fixed line of indication" or form a "restraining" or "overriding" judgment. Actors commit substantially violent criminal acts in the first and third cases, but not in the second one. Speaking facetiously, Robert Lejeune (1981) restated this finding as follows: "In other words and speaking plainly, if a person bent on committing a violent act changes his or her mind, a violent act will not occur" (p. 156). In

Lejeune's attempt to trivialize my finding, he ignored the larger theoretical context in which I embedded it (see chaps. 4 and 5). At the time the prevailing view was the still-popular one that violent criminal conduct does not take place through an interpretive process and consequently does not involve any significant amount of conscious calculation on the part of the criminal. It was believed that if violent criminals really thought about what they were doing, they would never commit their violent crimes. This naive belief was and still is based on the false assumption that unless violent criminals think like professional criminologists, their acts are, ipso facto, devoid of thought. The perpetuation of such ideas among criminologists, alias "social pathologists," suggests that these academicians still suffer from the lingering effects of the middle-class bias about which C. Wright Mills (1943) rightfully complained a half-century ago.

Third, this more detailed study led unexpectedly to my discovery of a new type of self-conception—an "incipiently violent" one (Athens 1977; see also chap. 6). The discovery of this third type of self-conception partially invalidated the proposition that I had formulated in my earlier study concerning the relationship between the self-conceptions of violent persons and their interpretations of violent situations. It thus forced me to reformulate this relationship, which constituted my fourth major finding (see chap. 7). The more complex relationship that I was forced to formulate covered cases in which individuals held all three types of self-conceptions:

> People who hold nonviolent self-images will commit violent criminal acts only in situations in which they form physically defensive interpretations. Those holding incipiently violent self-images will commit violent criminal acts only in situations in which they form physically defensive or frustrative-malefic interpretations. Finally, those holding violent self-images commit violent criminal acts in situations in which they form physically defensive or any one of the three offensive interpretations. (See chap. 9.)

The final major finding of my study concerned the careers of violent criminals (see chap. 8). In Evert Hughes's (1937) apt words, I pictured a violent career as a "moving perspective in which the person sees his life as a whole and interprets the meaning of his various attributes, actions, and the things which happen to him" (pp. 409–10). Similarly, in the often-cited book *Criminal Behavior Systems,* Clinard, Quinney, and Wildeman (1994) included in their conception of a criminal's career "his or her conception of self, his or her progression in criminal activity, and his or her identification with crime" (p. 14). Thus, in my examination of violent careers, I looked for changes in the way that people perceived being violent, changes in their self-conceptions, and changes in their participation in violent criminal acts.

I found that the careers of violent criminals fall into three fundamental types: "stable," "escalating," and "de-escalating." In stable careers the self-conceptions of the actors, as well as the types and amounts of violent acts committed by them, stay basically the same. Two subtypes of stable careers were also found: "violent" and "nonviolent" (see chap. 8). In the stable violent subtype, the self-conceptions and actions remain violent throughout the individuals' lives, whereas in the nonviolent stable subtype, the self-conceptions and actions remain nonviolent. In escalating violent careers, the self-conceptions of the individuals become progressively more violent as the kinds of violent acts that they committed become more serious and the violent acts become more frequent.

Finally, in de-escalating careers, the reverse happens: the self-conceptions of the individuals become progressively less violent as the kinds of violent acts that they commit become less serious and the violent acts become less frequent. My participant observation of nonincarcerated violent criminals (see appendix 2) was responsible for my spotting the de-escalating violent criminal career. Because people undergoing de-escalating violent careers commit fewer and fewer violent crimes over time, it is not surprising that I found no people who had undergone this type of career among the incarcerated subjects.

What I have spoken of here as a de-escalating violent career could represent a specific instance of what David Matza calls "maturational reform" in his book *Delinquency and Drift* (1963, pp. 22–26). Nevertheless maturing must be seen as an ongoing process that results from the lessons taught by life, which do not stop when adulthood is reached but continue until life ends. Thus maturational reform, and a de-escalating violent career, could occur during any phase of the violent criminal's life.

I drew two major conclusions from this second study. The first conclusion was that people who commit substantially violent acts have different generalized others. Individuals who hold violent self-conceptions have an. "unmitigated violent generalized other," an other that provides them with pronounced and categorical support for acting violently toward people. Individuals who hold incipiently violent self-conceptions have a "mitigated violent generalized other," an other that provides them with pronounced but limited categorical support for acting violently toward people. Finally, individuals who hold nonviolent self-conceptions have a "nonviolent generalized other," an other that does not provide them with any pronounced, categorical support for acting violently toward people, except in the case of defending themselves or loved ones from physical attack (Athens 1977, 1986, pp. 375–80; see also chap. 9).

After the completion of this study, however, for reasons explained elsewhere (Athens 1995), I replaced Mead's famous idea of the "generalized other" with my notion of the "phantom community" (Athens 1994, pp. 525–26). Both the generalized other and the phantom others refer to the interlocutors with whom we routinely consult when forming our self-conceptions or the interpretations of situations that confront us. Thus our self-conceptions are related to our interpretations of conflictive situations because in constructing both of them, we rely on advice from the same consultants (Athens 1994, pp. 527–28).

Nonetheless there is an important difference between Mead's notion of the generalized other and my notion of the phantom community. The perspective of the generalized other is the common perspective that, according to Mead, we derive from our community at large, whereas the phantom community's perspective is the one we derive from our past significant social experiences, which may be different from those of our present corporal community's members (Athens 1994, pp. 529–30). Thus even people living within the boundaries of the same corporal community may have different phantom communities, an existential circumstance to which Mead paid insufficient attention. Since the phantom companions that constitute our phantom communities travel with us wherever we go, we can always avail ourselves, for better or worse, of their counsel, no matter what corporal communities we may be inhabiting at the time. Consequently I must revise the original conclusion of my study from the claim that people who commit substantially violent acts have "unmitigated," "mitigated" or "nonviolent" generalized others to the claim that they have these same three types of phantom others.

The second major conclusion that I drew from my study was that people may change their phantom communities—formerly generalized others—over time and that changes in their phantom communities are responsible for the type of violent career they undergo (see chap. 8). In the case of escalating careers, individuals develop mitigated violent phantom communities and then unmitigated violent phantom ones. As the composition of their phantom community goes through these changes, the individuals expand the range and character of the situations that they interpret as calling for violence on their part, committing more substantially violent acts and eventually developing violent self-conceptions.

What is the underlying dynamic that changes the phantom communities of the individuals who are caught up in escalating violent careers? The person is confronted by situations in which he forms physically defensive interpretations. His success in taking violent actions in these conflictive situations leads his present significant others to consider him more violent and to show him more deference than before. If he accepts their new, more violent definition of himself and enjoys the new, more deferential way that they treat him, then he will develop an incipiently violent self-conception and, more important, a mitigated phantom community. He is now ready to take violent actions in situations in which he forms frustrative-malefic or physically defensive interpretations, whereas earlier he was prepared to act violently only in situations in which he formed physically defensive interpretations. In the wake of this development, he modifies his social circle and may change his immediate corporal community so that it includes more violent members.

Later this same actor is confronted by situations in which he forms frustrative-malefic interpretations. His success in taking violent actions in these conflictive situations prompts his significant others to perceive him to be even more violent than they had before and, accordingly, to display trepidation in his presence. If he accepts their newly revised, more violent definition of himself and welcomes the new wariness with which they approach him, then he will undergo a metamorphosis. He will develop not only a violent self-conception but, more important, an unmitigated phantom community. He is now prepared to take violent actions in conflictive situations in which he forms either physically defensive, pure frustrative, pure malefic, or frustrative-malefic interpretations. In the aftermath of this personal transformation, he once again modifies his social circle and may change his immediate corporal community to include even more violent members.

In the case of de-escalating careers, individuals with unmitigated violent phantom communities develop mitigated violent communities and then finally nonviolent ones. As the compositions of their phantom communities change, the actors constrain the range and character of situations that they interpret as calling for violence on their part, commit less substantially violent acts, and eventually develop nonviolent self-conceptions.

The underlying dynamic that changes the phantom communities of people undergoing de-escalating violent careers is the reverse of that in escalating violent careers. The critical moments in the development of the latter careers are acts of commission, whereas those in the development of the former are acts of omission. The individual is confronted by situations in which he forms pure frustrative or pure malefic interpretations but repeatedly fails to take successful violent actions in those situations for either of two reasons: he takes violent action but loses the battle against his antagonist, or he does not act violently toward his antagonist because he has formed a restraining judgment. In either case his repeated failure to take successful violent actions in these situations has dramatic repercussions. It leads his significant others to consider him less violent and to act more boldly toward him than they had before. If he accepts their newly revised definition of himself and tolerates their new, bolder way of approaching him, he will develop an incipiently violent self-conception and, more important, a mitigated violent phantom community. He will now act violently only in situations in which he forms physically defensive or frustrative-malefic interpretations. In the wake of this development, he modifies his social circle, if possible changing his immediate corporal community so that it will include fewer violent members.

When forming frustrative-malefic interpretations, this individual either is once again unsuccessful in taking violent actions or forms a restraining judgment that prevents him from acting violently. Consequently his significant others further revise their perceptions of him as an even less violent person and act even more boldly toward him. If he accepts their new definition of himself and tolerates their bolder way of approaching him, he will undergo a metamorphosis that brings about his development of a nonviolent self-conception and, more important, a nonviolent phantom community. He is now prepared to take violent actions only in conflictive situations in which he forms physically defensive interpretations. In the aftermath of this personal transformation, he once again modifies his social circle, if possible changing his immediate corporal community so that it will include few, if any, violent members.

Employing a conception of a criminal career in stark contrast to the one that guided my analysis, positivistic criminologists use a bowdlerized conception that, paradoxically, completely ignores the individual's changing interpretations of the real-life situations in which he will commit crimes, his changing perspectives toward the commission of crime in general, and his changing conceptions of himself. Instead they devote attention to those aspects of criminal careers that are easily quantifiable and therefore can be translated into neat mathematical formulas. In an article entitled "Characterizing Criminal Careers," which appeared in the prestigious magazine *Science*, Alfred Blumstein and Jacqueline Cohen (1987) reduce the careers of "active" criminals to the following set of algebraic expressions: "Among active offenders, three fundamental parameters represent the simplest characterization of a career structure: (i) age of initiation, A_o; (ii) age at termination, A_n; and (iii) mean number of crimes committed per year while active, λ. An important parameter of the criminal career is thus the career length represented by the interval $T = A_n - A_o$. Also at any point in the career, A_t, we are interested in the residual career length, $T_r = A_n - A_t$" (p. 986). Blumstein and Cohen illustrate how their precisely defined "parameters" of a criminal career can be operationalized by way of a figure that they instructively explain as follows:

> Here the career begins at age A_o and the individual crime frequency rises immediately to λ, stays constant at that value for the duration of the career, and drops instantaneously to 0 at age A_n when the career is terminated. Obviously, variations on this basic structure are possible. There could be a finite rise time or termination period between the maximum crime frequency, λ, and 0. Over the course of an individual's career, λ could fluctuate stochastically around his true underlying rate; in addition, there could well be variation in the true underlying λ including the possibility of dropping to 0 for intermittent periods, and many other variations. All of these involve greater complexity and would require more elaborate assumptions. (p. 986)

Despite their sophisticated use of mathematical and statistical techniques, not to mention the most lavish support for criminological research available in the world, the authors were forced to concede that "it is also clear that the issues are quite complex and the causal connections are often elusive" (p. 991). Unfortunately their concession represents a gross understatement on their part. More than seventy years ago W. I. Thomas (1967 [1923]) warned criminologists that "taken in themselves statistics are nothing more than symptoms of unknown causal processes" (p. 244). Although Blumstein and Cohen do uncover some important statistical facts about criminal careers, these facts are destined to remain the symptoms of an unknown causal process as long as positivists continue to study criminal careers inside the narrow scientific framework of their approach (Blumer 1969, pp. 56–58). Former newspaper reporter Robert Park (1952), who later became a sociologist, sublimely states the difference between studying careers or life histories from an interpretive approach and doing so using a positivistic approach: "In one case we are like a man in the dark looking at the outside of the house and trying to guess what is going on within. In the other, we are like a man who opens the door and walks in, and has visible before him what previously he had merely guessed at" (p. 208).

15 The Principal Phase, II: The Larger

Theoretical Implications

Although it did not dawn on me at the time, in my study I had developed an empirically grounded, rudimentary theory of violent criminal behavior. This did not really sink in until, to my pleasant surprise, I noticed *Violent Criminal Acts and Actors* included on the recommended reading list of Vold and Bernard's *Theoretical Criminology* (1986), where the authors characterized my book as providing "a general theory of violent crime, based upon symbolic interactionism" (p. 268). The basic assumption behind my theory is that crime is a product of *social retardation.* Social retardation exists when people guide their actions toward themselves and others from the standpoint of an underdeveloped, primitive phantom community, an "us" that hinders them from cooperating in the ongoing social activities of their corporal community or the larger society in which it is embedded.

More than thirty years ago Marshall B. Clinard (1959) stated a still much overlooked point that has profound implications for criminology: "The act as well as the actor must be considered" (p. 519). I had failed to realize fully not only that I had developed a theory but also that my theory conforms with five brute facts about violent criminal acts and actors.

The first brute fact to which my theory conforms is that more than one type of violent criminal act exists. Since my theory portrays violent criminal acts as resulting from any one of four interpretations of conflictive situations, it implies that there are four distinct types of violent criminal acts: physically defensive, pure frustrative, pure malefic, and frustrative-malefic. It should be noted that the first type, the physically defensive violent criminal act, comprises violent acts that fail, for one reason or another, to meet the legal requirements for self-defense, so that as perfect instances of "imperfect self-defenses," they qualify as bona fide acts of criminal violence. Thus the brute fact that there are multiple types of violent criminal acts contradicts any theory in which all or most criminal violent acts are crammed into a single form, as is done in the case of the "character contest" model (Athens 1985; Luckenbill 1977; Ray and Simmons 1987).

It should be also noted that there are two subtypes of my frustrative type of violent criminal act. Frustrative violent criminal acts are products of "frustrative interpretations" of conflictive situations, which can be formed in either of two distinct ways (see chap. 4). First, by assuming the attitudes of his soon-to-be victims, the perpetrator of violence tells himself that the victims intend to resist the specific line of action that he wants to execute. Next, by assuming the attitude of his phantom community, he tells himself that he should respond violently toward the victims and calls out a violent plan of action from within himself. The other distinct way in which an individual can form a frustrative interpretation is as follows. First, by assuming his soon-to-be victims' attitudes, he tells himself that they want him to cooperate in a specific line of action that he does not want to carry out. Next, by assuming the attitude of his phantom community, he tells himself that he should respond violently, once again calling out a violent plan of action from within himself. The two ways that an individual can form a frustrative interpretation thus have the same second steps, but the initial steps differ, giving these acts a slightly different meaning for the actor and thereby creating two subtypes of the pure frustrative violent criminal acts. In the first, "coercive" subtype, the individual considers his violent plan of action to be the best means of overpowering other people's resistance to the larger act that he wants to carry out, such as sexual intercourse or robbery. In the second, "resistive" subtype, the individual sees his violent plan of action as the most effective way to block the larger act that other people want carried out but that he does not, such as divorce or arrest.

That there is more than one type of violent criminal is the second brute fact to which my theory conforms. According to my theory, three types of violent criminals can be distinguished on the basis of their phantom communities (formerly generalized others) and self-conceptions: (1) "marginally violent," (2) "violent," and (3) "ultraviolent." Ultraviolent criminals inhabit unmitigated violent phantom communities and paint violent portraits of themselves (see, for example, Dietz 1983; Katz 1988, pp. 218–36). Violent criminals inhabit mitigated violent phantom communities and paint incipiently violent self-portraits, whereas the marginally violent criminals inhabit nonviolent phantom communities and, naturally, paint only nonviolent portraits of themselves. Finally, each of these types of violent individuals stands on clearly different steps on a violence progression ladder. The marginally violent individual stands on the first rung, the violent individual stands on the middle rung, and the ultraviolent individual stands on the top rung (Athens 1986, pp. 375–80).

The third brute fact to which my theory conforms is that different types of violent criminals are capable of engaging in quite different types of violent criminal acts (Athens 1985, p. 430). If violent criminals are not equally violent, then common sense dictates that they should not commit the same kinds of violent criminal acts. According to my theory, ultraviolent criminals will commit physically defensive, pure frustrative, pure malefic, or frustrative-malefic violent criminal acts. Violent criminals will commit both physically defensive and frustrative-malefic violent criminal acts, whereas marginally violent ones will commit only physically defensive violent criminal acts (Athens 1986, pp. 375–80). Thus a comprehensive theory of violent criminals must explain the violence capability of each different type of violent criminal, not just the most violent type—the ultraviolent criminal—as Katz (1988), for example, does.

More than seven decades ago the famous sociological tandem of Robert Park and Ernest Burgess (1969 [1924]) originally drew the distinction between "expressive" and "positive," or instrumental, behavior: "A very much larger part of human behavior than we ordinarily imagine is merely expressive . . . activity carried out for its own sake. Only work, action which has some ulterior motive or is performed from a conscious sense of duty, falls wholly and without reservation into the second class" (p. 369). Four decades later the positivistic psychologist Arnold Buss (1961, pp. 1–16) distinguished "instrumental" from "angry," or expressive, aggression, a distinction that has subsequently become a standard part of psychologists', sociologists', and criminologists' vernacular. Instrumental aggression is only a means to another end, whereas angry aggression is the end in itself. Although using an obvious means/end scheme, Buss (1961) sought to avoid any reference to the aggressor's intention so as to cast his distinction as strictly as possible in positivistic terms:

> There are two reasons for excluding the concept of intent. . . . First, it implies teleology, a purposive act directed toward a future goal, and this view is inconsistent with the behavioral approach adopted in this book. Secondly, and more important, is the difficulty of applying this term to behavioral events. . . .

In summary, *intent* is both awkward and unnecessary in the analysis of aggressive behavior. (p. 2; emphasis in orginal)

In disavowing intention Buss becomes guilty of reductionism. He mistakenly reduces a social act to a purely physical act. About twenty years earlier Park (1938) humorously illustrated the nature of this mistake:

> If innocently . . . I am walking along the street and a brick falls on my head or close enough at least to interrupt my meditations, that in itself is a mere physical fact. If, however, looking up I see a face grinning down on me maliciously from the wall from which the brick came, the fall of the brick ceases to be a mere physical phenomenon and becomes a social fact. It changes its character as soon as I interpret it as an expression of an attitude or intent rather than an act of God . . . that is wholly without intention of any sort, and one therefore, for which no one can be made responsible. (p. 189)

In a much later and more enlightened discussion, Buss (1978) distinguishes instrumental aggression from angry aggression on the basis of "the stimuli that elicit them, the accompanying emotion, and the consequences" (p. 342) but still not on the basis of actors' varying interpretations of the conflictive situations that confront them:

> The first class, angry aggression, is commonly incited by insult, attack, or annoyances. The usual emotional reaction is anger. . . . The usual consequence of angry aggression is pain and discomfort of the victim; the intent of the aggressor is to harm the victim. . . . The second class, instrumental aggression, is caused by competition or by any of the usual incentives that motivate behavior (dominance, food, mate, . . .). There may be an emotional reaction (anger), but it is not a necessary part of the sequence. The usual consequence is success in competition or attainment of the incentive; any harm to the victim is incidental. (pp. 342–43)

If the interpretive process is included rather than excluded from Buss's classificatory scheme, then it can subsume the four types of violent criminal acts that I found my three different types of violent criminals to commit. More specifically, physically defensive and frustrative violent criminal acts are purely instrumental. Malefic violent criminal acts are purely expressive, and frustrative-malefic violent criminal acts are combined instrumental-expressive violent criminal acts. Because marginally violent criminals commit only physically defensive violent criminal acts, they engage in only purely instrumental extreme acts of aggression. Because violent criminals commit physically defensive and frustrative-malefic violent criminal acts, they engage in both purely instrumental and combined instrumental/expressive extreme acts of aggression. Finally, because ultra-violent criminals commit physically defensive, pure frustrative, pure malefic, and frustrative-malefic violent criminal acts, they engage in purely instrumental, purely expressive, and combined instrumental/expressive extreme acts of aggression. Classifying the violent criminal actors and acts distinguished in my theory on the basis of whether they engage in expressive or instrumental extreme acts of aggression demonstrates that only the most dangerous violent criminals will engage in purely expressive acts of extreme aggression. Thus, when revised, Buss's classification system adds a bit of insight to my findings.

The fourth brute fact to which my theory conforms is that violent criminal actors and acts are not evenly spread across the social landscape but pop up more frequently in some places than they do in others (Park 1952, pp. 46–49). According to Park (1952), every corporal community is "a mosaic of minor communities, many of them strikingly different from one another, but all more or less typical" (p. 196). He considers minor communities to be synonymous with "natural areas." In every natural area, or minor community, there are certain types of individuals whose impact on the flavor and tempo of their community's daily life far exceeds their absolute numbers (Wirth 1928, p. 286). Since conflict is indigenous to human group life, conflict inevitably breaks out between the members of any minor community. To varying degrees a community's members will inform one another about how conflicts are handled in their communities. Thus, on the basis of the nature of a community's predominant individual types and the prevailing wisdom for handling interpersonal conflicts, three kinds of communities can be demarcated: *civil, malignant,* and *turbulent.* In civil minor communities the predominant individual type is the marginally violent person, whose nonviolent phantom community is congruent with that of his minor community and the larger corporal community that encompasses it. Among the members of civil minor communities, the prevailing wisdom is that interpersonal conflicts should be handled by nonviolent means, such as gossiping about one another and ostracizing, snubbing, and avoiding each other. They will use physical violence only as a last resort when they are physically attacked and must do for themselves what the police cannot do at that moment. Violent criminal acts of any type thus occur rarely in such a community. Nevertheless, because the boundaries between different natural areas are permeable, individuals prone to greater violence may always wander into and occasionally try to settle in civil communities, making the threat of violent criminal acts a remote but ever-present possibility.

In malignant minor communities the predominant individual type is the ultraviolent person, whose unmitigated phantom community is congruent with that of his minor corporal community but in conflict with that of the larger corporal community of which it is part (Brown 1965; Canada 1995). Members of malignant communities know that the prevailing wisdom is that physical violence is the most effective means for handling serious conflicts. Any time a serious conflict arises, it is taken for granted that one must be prepared to use deadly force, as well as to be the recipient of it. The members of these communities live with the bleak realization that at any time they could become embroiled in a conflict in which they could either kill or be killed. The marginally violent individuals who become trapped in these communities must endure the harsh reality that they or one of their loved ones could at any time be added to their violent and ultraviolent neighbors' lists of victims, whereas violent individuals brace themselves for the inevitable day when they will clash with each other or one of their ultraviolent neighbors. As Elijah Anderson (1990) perceptively observes: "They must be on guard even against people they have known over many years" (p. 80). Thus malignant communities constitute virtual combat zones where violent criminal acts of all types—pure frustrative, pure malefic, frustrative-malefic, and physically defensive—occur with such depressing frequency that they become commonplace.

A young man laments the extraordinary safety precautions that his mother must take to survive in the malignant community in which she lives:

> My mother goes through a lot of changes, just to live from day to day. . . . I remember when she got a new fridge one time, she just cut the box up and put out a little each week. . . . She didn't want her neighbors to know she'd gotten something, because that meant either she had money or there was something in there to steal. . . .
>
> And whenever she'd go to church, she would put her pocketbook over her shoulder, and then put her coat on over the pocket book. . . . And no jewelry. Even if she was gonna get a ride. . . . She'd wait till she got in the car, and then on the way to where she was going put it on. On the way back, she'd take it off. It's a hell of a way to live, but that's how she avoided problems. (Anderson 1990, pp. 78–79)

In contrast to the situation in both civil and malignant communities, in turbulent minor communities no individual type has gained the upper hand, so that there is no predominant individual type but instead an admixture of types. Thus ultraviolent people with their unmitigated violent phantom communities, violent people with their mitigated violent phantom communities, and marginally violent people with their nonviolent phantom communities all come to live, work, and play in close physical proximity with one another. The odd mixture of uncongenial individual types that characterizes turbulent communities creates a social environment where, as Park (1952) says, "everything is loose and free, but everything is problematic" (p. 89). There exists, therefore, no prevailing wisdom for handling interpersonal conflicts among members of these communities. Conflict arises not only over this or that particular issue but also over the appropriate means for their resolution. Since community members are not sure what to expect when conflicts erupt, life in the community is chaotic. This creates the potentially dangerous situation that Park describes in his foreword to *The Gold Coast and the Slum* as being one "in which the physical distances and the social distances do not coincide; a situation in which people who live side by side are not, and—because of the divergence of their interests and their heritages—cannot, even with the best of good will, become neighbors" (rpt. in Park 1952, pp. 89–90). Thus, as expected, sundry violent criminal acts occur more frequently in turbulent communities than in civil communities, although much less frequently than in malignant communities.

In *Street Wise* Anderson (1990) succinctly but sublimely describes a turbulent community that he dubs the "Village":

> A perfunctory look at the Village streets in daytime would lead one to believe that this is indeed a pleasant neighborhood whose residents get along well, and that there is genuine comity among the various kinds of people who live there. And to a large extent this is true. As residents stroll up and down the tree-lined streets, there is often a pleasant show of civility, if not intimacy, between neighbors. . . .
>
> Yet many residents are concerned about the strangers with whom they must share the public space, including wandering homeless people, aggressive beggars, muggers, anonymous black youths, and drug addicts. . . .
>
> Increasingly, people see the streets as a jungle, especially at night. . . . They are then on special alert, carefully monitoring every-

one who passes and giving few people the benefit of the doubt. . . .
Although there is a general need to view the Village as an island of
civility . . . the underlying sense is that the local streets and public
spaces are uncertain at best and hostile at worst. (pp. 237–39)

Social segregation is the common social process through which all three
of these different minor communities, or natural areas, are created. According to Park (1952), "The natural areas into which the urban—and every other type of community, in fact—resolves itself are, at least, in the first instance,
the products of a sifting and sorting process which we may call segregation"
(p. 199). Blumer (1956b) points out that "segregation is a primary means by
which a human society develops an inner organization" (p. 137). "One can
say," he adds, "that the process of segregation in one form or another is accepted, employed, and condoned by all human societies" (p. 138).

Although operating on a large-scale basis and producing long-lasting
consequences, social segregation is ultimately a product of people's interpretations of a recurrent problem (Blumer 1969, pp. 57–59, 108, 1981, pp.
160–61). Because people must always live somewhere, the problem becomes where to lay their hats and rest their heads. They must separately
or jointly decide where it is best for people to reside given their life cir-
cumstances. In deciding on a minor community or neighborhood in which
to settle, they may take into account a whole array of factors, including the
cost of housing, the reputation of the schools, the proximity to public trans-
portation, and the physical distance to their present or anticipated places
of employment, as well as the social distance between them and their likely
neighbors (Blumer 1956b, p. 137). Although all these factors will be important in this decision, none will be any more important than the fear of
violent crime. Rich, poor, or in-between, few people would wish to move
into or long remain in a community where they would likely brush shoulders with violent and ultraviolent criminals (see, for example, Anderson
1990, pp. 55, 65, 76–78, 138–45, 154–55, 248–49).

Nevertheless the communities created from this social segregation process are not static entities that, once formed, never change. On the contrary
they are always evolving by moving back and forth from a state of relative
stability to one of transition (McKenzie 1971 [1924], pp. 22–32). As ultraviolent criminals invade civil communities and marginally violent people
flee from them, these communities slowly degenerate into malignant ones.
Likewise, as ultraviolent criminals are driven from malignant communities and marginally violent people move into them, the community progressively becomes more civil. Turbulent communities are those that are

caught in the middle of this larger process of community change. They represent communities in which, in Park's (1952) apt words, "the old order is passing, but the new order has not yet arrived" (p. 89). Thus turbulent communities are either in transition from civil into malignant communities or from malignant into civil communities.

Park (1952, pp. 223–32) views social segregation and the community change that it brings about as occurring inside the larger social process of "succession":

> Although the term succession, as originally employed by sociologists, would seem to be more appropriately applied to movements of population and to such incidental social and cultural changes as these movements involve, there seems to be no sound reason why the same term should not be used to describe any orderly and *irreversible series of events,* provided they are to such an extent correlated with other less obvious and more fundamental social changes that they may be used as indices of these changes. (p. 224; emphasis added)

Later he formally defines succession as follows: "Changes, when they are recurrent, so that they fall into a temporal or spatial series—particularly if the series is of such a sort that the effect of each succeeding increment of change reinforces or carries forward the effects of the proceeding—constitute what is described in this paper as succession" (p. 229).

Contrary to Park's notion of succession, community change is a precarious process capable of reversing direction. Unforeseen contingencies can always arise that affect the course of a community's life no less than the lives of the individuals who inhabit it (see, for example, Anderson 1990, pp. 152–55). A civil community that changes into a turbulent one may always revert to a civil one without becoming a malignant one. The invasion of ultraviolent criminals into a civil community may always be halted before they become the predominant individual type. Likewise a malignant community that becomes a turbulent one may always revert to a malignant one without becoming a civil one. Marginally violent people may always be frightened away before they can establish a beachhead and later become the predominant individual type in a malignant community. In both instances the succession process is rudely interrupted before it reaches the expected destination. Moreover, before the ultimate direction of a turbulent community's further evolution becomes apparent, the community may stay in its present state for a long period (See, for example, Anderson 1990, pp. 26, 30, 150–51, 162).

In all fairness, I must admit that Park (1952) recognized the problems with his use of succession to explain community change. In an attempt to salvage the idea, he broadened his earlier definition to include the forms of community change that happen in civil, turbulent, and malignant communities: "In view, however, of the complexity of social change . . . it seems desirable to include within the perspective and purview of the concept, and of studies of succession, every possible form of orderly change so far as it affects the interrelations of individuals in a community or the structure of the society of which these individuals are part" (pp. 229–30).

Unfortunately there are limits to which the meaning of any concept can be stretched before its meaning is lost. The idea of succession clearly implies that communities change over an endless cycle or series of irreversible stages. It does not merely imply, as Park belatedly suggests, any change that follows an orderly process. To the contrary, it definitely implies a particular kind of orderly process of change, where one stage inevitably comes after another in an irreversible sequence. Consequently the notion should be discarded.

The fifth and final brute fact about violent criminal acts and actors to which my theory conforms is that both may change over time by becoming either more or less violent. The latter, salutary development takes place in the case of de-escalating violent careers, and the former, unfortunate one takes place in the case of escalating violent ones. In retrospect I also discovered that the stable "violent" career, a subtype of the more general stable career, is merely a methodological artifact (Athens 1992, pp. 21–26). My second study included many middle-aged offenders who, because of the sheer amount of elapsed time, were simply unable to recall much about the earlier periods of their lives when they held nonviolent self-conceptions and had not performed any substantially violent acts. I had created this erroneous subtype on the basis of my study of their cases. Thus I mistakenly classified these violent criminals as undergoing stable violent careers when, undoubtedly, they had undergone escalating ones (Athens 1992).

Although slow to recognize that I had developed a new theory congruent with the five brute facts about violent criminal acts and actors just described, I recognized immediately that female violent criminals did not constitute an anomaly as far as this theory is concerned. Because I had strategically used female violent offenders in constructing the theory, my explanation could account for women's violent crimes. In fact including women in my second study was responsible for my discovery that violent criminal actors can have mitigated violent phantom communities (formerly generalized others) and incipiently violent self-conceptions. Their inclusion also helped me to discover that these phantom communities, and to a lesser extent self-images, play a pivotal part in a normal progression through an escalating and de-escalating violent criminal career.

16 The Principal Phase, III: The Policy Implications

A theory with no policy implications is sterile, whereas a policy not guided by any explicit theory is foolhardy. Implementing a policy that is not based explicitly on some theory is like driving to a distant, unknown destination without a road map. Unfortunately the theory of violent crime that I develop here is far from complete, so that it would be impossible to derive a full-blown and detailed policy for the control of violent crime from it. Nevertheless, based on the theory's present state of development, I can at least roughly outline a policy. The policy would blend mainly general prevention, selective rehabilitation, and selective incapacitation. Although deterrence and retribution are not key ingredients, they are part of the recipe.

The policy would also be tailored to the communities, both corporal and phantom, in which the violent criminal actor and act are bred. In malignant communities it would call for the initiation of a general prevention program. Its main goal would be to foster development of nonviolent phantom communities and to stymie development of unmitigated violent ones, so that their members' phantom communities would be congruent with those of their larger corporal community. This would be achieved through a broad-based education program that would emphasize teaching people not only how to read, write, and compute but also, and equally important, how to fulfill their general duties and obligations as community members. Park (1952) describes the logic on which this broad-based, community-oriented education program would operate: "The community, including the family, with its wider interests, its larger purposes, and its more deliberate aims, surrounds us, incloses us, and compels us to conform; not by mere pressure from without, not by fear of censure merely, but by the sense of our interest in, and responsibility to, certain interest not our own" (p. 57).

Nevertheless this broad-based, community-oriented education program would always include specific instruction about the laws that govern using both deadly and nondeadly force in general, as well as those that govern using any force whatsoever, particularly in sexual relations. There is a dire need to counteract the ideas circulating in the community about people's right to act violently toward one another. A community-oriented education program would also include feeding hungry students, because students whose minds are on their stomachs cannot be expected to concentrate on their computers.

Park (1952) observes that "neither the orphan asylum nor any other agency has thus far succeeded in providing a wholly satisfactory substitute for the home" (p. 58). Although this observation remains as true today as when first made more than seventy years ago, the community can provide schools that socialize their students more effectively. Schools must be expected to perform this function, even when parents fail to perform their part of this bargain adequately. In *The Unadjusted Girl* W. I. Thomas (1967 [1923]) summarizes the crux of my position: "It is desirable that the school should eventually supersede the juvenile court and replace other welfare agencies concerned with the child, but in adapting itself to this task and to the task of general education it will be compelled to make provision for the development of the emotional and social life of the child as well as the informational" (p. 221).

Although the community cannot guarantee a good family to every child, it can guarantee them a good school. A good school can go a long way in making up for a bad family, as Thomas (1967) concluded more than seven decades ago: "If we invented any device to replace social influence lacking at other points it would be the school. It is probable that the school could be sort of a community forming the background of the family and the child and could supply the elements lacking in the home, at least to the degree of preventing in a large measure delinquency and crime, if it exercised all the influence it could conceivably exercise, and that it could, more than any other agency, socialize the family" (p. 214).

The school not only should act as the primary vehicle for the community's crime-prevention program through its broad-based, community-oriented educational instruction but also should serve as a feeder for the community's selective rehabilitative programs. "It is quite impossible psychologically to hate the sin and love the sinner," Mead interjects (1964,

p. 228). He importantly adds that "to understand is to forgive" (p. 228). It is not only possible but desirable for the members of a community to forgive newly created violent criminals for committing minor physically defensive or frustrative-malefic violent criminal acts and to seek, with their cooperation, to rehabilitate them before they become ultraviolent criminals and commit far more serious violent crimes. Since violent people usually develop mitigated phantom communities at least by the time they leave middle school, teachers are in a strategic position to identify them based on their misconduct at school. This identification is vitally important because the opportunity for rehabilitation can be made available to these individuals while they still have a real chance to benefit from it (Athens 1992, p. 93).

The ultraviolent criminals in our communities are outside the reach of any presently devisable long-term rehabilitation programs, much less short-term ones. Their placement in these programs would endanger not only the staff of such programs but also the other participants (Athens 1992, p. 96). Ultraviolent criminals have already committed at least some serious physically defensive or frustrative-malefic violent criminal acts, and possibly some serious pure malefic or frustrative ones. Contrary to Mead's advice (1964, pp. 226–39), the community can no longer safely afford to look away and to forgive either these individuals or their violent criminal acts. If these violent criminals were allowed to escape the harsh punishment that they deserve for their crimes, it would undermine the larger corporal community's legitimacy in the eyes of its nonviolent members (Erickson 1966, pp. 8–13). Speaking metaphorically, the community must now hate both the sin and the sinner. Since such individuals have already developed into ultraviolent criminals, since they cannot now be rehabilitated with certain success, and since they have already done grave harm to people, they should be prevented from seriously hurting any more community members by having them serve lengthy prison sentences.

As long as ultraviolent criminals roam freely about the streets and schools and continue their unbridled attacks on community members, no general prevention or selective rehabilitation will ever succeed. The predatory violent actions of ultraviolent criminals will either prevent the educational and rehabilitative programs from realizing their goals or negate any gains that may be achieved through their implementation (see Canada 1995, pp. 25–26, 108–9). Community members will have little faith in education or rehabilitation programs when they and their neighbors are daily subjected to the threat of murder, rape, robbery, and assault.

Thus the success of these educational and rehabilitation programs will hinge on the removal of ultraviolent criminals from the community. Since ultraviolent criminals cannot be removed from the community for a lengthy period of time until they are convicted of serious felonies, the criminal justice system would have to mount a concerted effort to secure the necessary convictions against these individuals.

The telltale sign that a member of the community is an ultraviolent criminal is his commission of either a pure frustrative or malefic serious violent criminal act. By carefully considering the details of the incident in which a violent crime occurred, a police officer, district attorney, or judge could determine whether a pure malefic or frustrative violent crime was committed and thereby whether the suspect or defendant is an ultraviolent criminal. On the basis of this determination, they would then target his case for more stringent handling. More specifically, police officers would target him for special investigation and arrest, district attorneys would target him for the severest possible prosecution, and judges would target him for the harshest possible sentence (Moore, Estrich, McGillis, and Spelmon 1984, pp. 95–180).

In contrast to the situation in malignant communities, the problem in civil communities is not the initiation of a successful general prevention program but its continuation. Once the ball gets rolling, it needs to be pushed to achieve the desired results. The development of marginally violent community members, whose nonviolent phantom communities are congruent with those of the larger corporal community, can be never taken for granted. Thus, once started, a community cannot rest on its laurels but must continue to play an active part in shaping its younger members' phantom communities into nonviolent ones. The realization of this goal requires the continuous effective instruction of its younger members for living in the adult civil community. Park (1952) poignantly depicts the hoped-for end result of this preparation process: "Only gradually, as he succeeds in accommodating himself to the life of the larger group, incorporating into the specific purposes and ambitions of his own life the larger and calmer purposes of the society in which he lives, does the individual . . . find himself quite at home in the community in which he is part" (p. 57).

Reaching this goal would require continuing the effective operation of the previously described general prevention, selective rehabilitation, and selective incapacitation programs. However, the careful monitoring of these programs by citizens' watchdog groups would be necessary to guarantee their ongoing effective operation. Community members would have to be alert for any decline in their schools' and criminal justice agencies' implementation of these programs, and they would have to monitor the agencies continuously to ensure that the larger interests of the community were not being sacrificed for the narrower organizational interests of these agencies. Bureaucratization would sound the death knell for the successful operation of these community programs and the violent crime control policy from which they evolved.

Although discounting the operation of deterrence altogether from the violent crime-control policy outlined thus far would be a grave mistake, it would be an even graver mistake to emphasize deterrence more than general prevention, selective rehabilitation, or selective incapacitation. People are more likely to refrain from violence out of preference for a nonviolent existence than they are to do so out of fear of punishment (see Canada 1995, pp. 159–60). Fear of punishment is only one of several important reasons for forming restraining judgments that may stop people from committing some particular violent criminal acts, but it will not necessarily stop them permanently from committing all violent criminal acts (see chap. 5). Unless marginally violent, violent, or ultraviolent individuals repeatedly form restraining judgments out of fear of punishment, neither special nor general deterrence, whatever the particular case may be, will by itself stop escalating violent criminal careers or start de-escalating ones. Of course, a police officer on every block around the clock would be required for such a deterrence policy to have any hope of success.

Once ultraviolent criminals successfully invade and become the predominant individual type in a community, it can be too late to halt a community's decline. There will be a mass exodus of the marginally violent people from the community. A social vacuum will be then created, paving the way for the impending invasion of even more violent and ultraviolent people. The turbulent community is born in the aftermath of this social segregation, or sorting process. Thus the best policy for its eradication is the effective implementation of the previously advocated programs for the control of violent criminals in other communities. If the problem of violent crime were satisfactorily eliminated in malignant communities and effectively squelched in civil ones, then people would no longer need to migrate from one community to another in search of a safe place in which they and their families could live. Fear of crime and bad schools would then cease to exist as motives for social segregation.

17 Final Thoughts

I did not recognize that I had developed a theory of violent criminal behavior in this tiny book until long after it was published. Thus the explanation that I had originally developed between its narrow covers was more
implicit than explicit. Since I provided only the bare skeleton of a theory,
with very little flesh or connective tissue between the bones, I shot myself
in the proverbial foot. One has to read carefully between the lines to get
any inkling that I had developed a theory, which made it easy for positivists, or for that matter criminologists of any theoretical persuasion, to dis-
miss the contribution of my book without a second thought. The book's
republication has given me the opportunity to rehabilitate it by explicitly
making the theoretical points that I had made only implicitly before, as well
as to develop some of its policy implications. Although at first I despised
the task because I associated it with failure, after I finally started it, I experienced a new feeling, one that Thomas Wolfe (1936) sublimely captures
in *The Story of a Novel:*

> It was as if I had discovered a whole new universe of chemical ele-
> ments and had began to see certain relations between some of them
> but had by no means began to organize the whole series into a har-
> monious and coherent union. From this time on, I think my efforts
> might be described as the effort to complete that organization, to
> discover that articulation for which I strove, to bring about that final
> coherent union. I know that I have failed thus far in doing so, but I
> believe that I understand pretty thoroughly just where the nature of
> my failure lies, and of course my deepest and most earnest hope is
> that the time will come when I shall not fail. (pp. 35–36)

To the extent that I have succeeded in rehabilitating my book, its contribution to the field of criminology can now be judged more easily. Thus the true degree of my success or failure in explaining violent criminality can be less easily denied by myself or, more important, by others.

Works Cited

Abrahamsen, David. 1960. *The psychology of crime.* New York: Columbia
University Press.

Akers, Ronald. 1994. *Criminological theories.* Los Angeles: Roxbury.

Amir, Menachem. 1971. *Patterns in forcible rape.* Chicago: University of
Chicago Press.

Anderson, Elijah. 1990. *Street wise.* Chicago: University of Chicago Press.

Athens, Lonnie. 1974. The self and the violent criminal act. *Urban Life and
Culture* 3:98–112.

———. 1977. Violent crime: A symbolic interactionist study. *Symbolic Interaction* 1:56–70.

———. 1980. *Violent criminal acts and actors: A symbolic interactionist
study.* London: Routledge and Kegan Paul.

———. 1984a. Blumer's method of naturalistic inquiry: A critical examination. In *Studies in symbolic interaction,* vol. 5, ed. Norman K. Denzin,
241–57. Greenwich, Conn.: JAI.

———. 1984b. Scientific criteria for evaluating qualitative studies. In *Studies in symbolic interaction,* vol. 5, ed. Norman K. Denzin, 259–68.
Greenwich, Conn.: JAI.

———. 1985. Character contests and violent criminal conduct: A critique.
The Sociological Quarterly 26:419–34.

———. 1986. Types of violent persons: Toward the development of a symbolic interactionist theory of violent criminal behavior. In *Studies in
symbolic interaction,* vol. 7B, ed. Norman K. Denzin, 367–89. Greenwich, Conn.: JAI.

———. 1992. *The creation of dangerous violent criminals.* Urbana: University of Illinois Press.

———. 1993a. Blumer's advanced social psychology course. In *Studies in
symbolic interaction,* vol. 14, ed. Norman K. Denzin, 155–62. Greenwich, Conn.: JAI.

———. 1993b. Blumer's advanced course on social psychology. In *Studies in symbolic interaction,* vol. 14, ed. Norman K. Denzin, 163–93. Greenwich, Conn.: JAI.

———. 1994. The self as a soliloquy. *The Sociological Quarterly* 35:521–532.

———. 1995. Mead's visions of the self: A pair of flawed diamonds. In *Studies in symbolic interaction,* vol. 18, ed. Norman K. Denzin, 245–61. Greenwich, Conn.: JAI.

Ball-Rokeach, Sandra. 1973. Values and violence: A test of the subculture of violence thesis. *American Sociological Review* 38:736–49.

Banay, Ralph. 1952. Study in murder. *The Annals of the American Academy of Political and Social Sciences* 284:26–34.

Becker, Howard. 1953. Becoming a marihuana user. *American Journal of Sociology* 59:235–42.

———. 1966. Introduction. In C. Shaw, *The jack-roller,* v–xviii. Chicago: University of Chicago Press.

———. 1973. *Outsiders.* New York: Free Press.

Bensing, Robert, and Oliver Schroeder Jr. 1960. *Homicide in an urban community.* Springfield, Ill.: Charles Thomas.

Berry, People vs. 18 Cal. 3d 509, 556 P. 2d 777 (1976).

Bjerre, Andreas. 1927. *The psychology of murder.* London: Longmans, Green.

Blumer, Herbert. 1929. Method in social psychology. Ph.D. diss., Department of Sociology, University of Chicago.

———. 1937. Social psychology. In *Man and society,* ed. E. Schmidt, 148–98. Englewood Cliffs, N.J.: Prentice-Hall.

———. 1940. The problem of the concept in social psychology. *American Journal of Sociology* 45:707–19.

———. 1954. What is wrong with social theory. *American Sociological Review* 19:3–10.

———. 1956a. Sociological analysis and the "variable." *American Sociological Review* 21:683–90.

———. 1956b. Social science and the desegregation process. *The Annals of the American Academy of Political and Social Science* 304:137–43.

———. 1962. Society as symbolic interaction. In *Human behavior and social processes,* ed. A. Rose, 179–92. Boston: Houghton Mifflin.

———. 1967. Threats from agency—determined research: The case of Camelot. In *The rise and fall of Project Camelot,* ed. I. Horowitz, 153–74. Cambridge, Mass.: MIT Press.

———. 1969. *Symbolic interactionism: Perspective and method.* Englewood Cliffs, N.J.: Prentice-Hall.

———. 1975. Symbolic interaction and the idea of social system. *Revue Internationale de Sociologie* 11:3–12.

————. 1980. Foreword. In Lonnie Athens, *Violent criminal acts and actors: A symbolic interactionist study,* ix–xii. London: Routledge and Kegan Paul.

————. 1981. George Herbert Mead. In *The future of the sociological classics,* ed. B. Rhea, 136–69. London: Allen and Unwin.

Blumstein, Alfred, and Jacqueline Cohen. 1987. Characterizing criminal careers. *Science* 237:985–91.

Brown, Claude. 1965. *Manchild in the promised land.* New York: Signet.

Buss, Alfred. 1961. *The psychology of aggression.* New York: Wiley.

————. 1978. *Psychology: Behavior in perspective.* New York: Wiley.

Canada, Geoffrey. 1995. *Fist stick knife gun: A personal history of violence in America.* Boston: Beacon.

Carrol, James, and Gerald Fuller. 1971. An MMPI comparison of three groups of criminals. *Journal of Clinical Psychology* 27:240–42.

Chappell, Duncan, and Susan Singer. 1977. Rape in New York City: A study of material in the police files and its meaning. In *Forcible rape: The crime, the victim, and the offender,* ed. D. Chappell, R. Geis, and G. Geis, 249–71. New York: Columbia University Press.

Cicourel, Aaron. 1964. *Method and measurement in sociology.* Glencoe, Ill.: Free Press.

Clinard, Marshall. 1959. Criminological research. In *Sociology today: Problems and prospects,* vol. 2, ed. R. Merton, L. Broom, and L. Cottrell Jr., 509–36. New York: Harper and Row.

————. 1966. The sociologist's quest for respectability. *The Sociological Quarterly* 7:399–412.

Clinard, Marshall, Richard Quinney, and John Wildeman. 1994. *Criminal behavior systems.* Cincinnati: Anderson.

Cole, K. E., Gary Fisher, and Shirely Cole. 1968. Women who kill: A sociopsychological study. *Archives of General Psychiatry* 19:14.

Cooley, Charles. 1926. The roots of social knowledge. *American Journal of Sociology* 32:59–79.

Cressey, Donald. 1953. *Other people's money.* New York: Free Press.

Curran, Daniel, and Claire Renzetti. 1994. *Theories of crime.* Boston: Allyn and Bacon.

Curtis, Lynn. 1974. *Criminal violence.* Lexington, Ky.: Heath.

Cuthbertson, Beverly, and John Johnson. 1992. Exquisite emotional sensitivity and capture. In *Studies in symbolic interaction,* vol. 13, ed. Norman K. Denzin, 155–66. Greenwich, Conn.: JAI.

Denzin, Norman. 1984. Toward a phenomenology of domestic family violence. *American Journal of Sociology* 90:483–513.

————. 1985. On the phenomenology of sexuality, desire, and violence. *Current Perspectives in Social Theory* 6:39–56.

————. 1986. *On understanding emotion.* San Francisco: Jossey-Bass.

166   Works Cited

———. 1987. *The alcoholic self.* Newbury Park, Calif.: Sage.

———. 1989. *Interpretive interactionism.* Newbury Park, Calif.: Sage.

Deutscher, Irwin. 1970. Buchenwald, Mai Lai, and Charles Van Doren: Social psychology as explanation. *The Sociological Quarterly* 11:533–40.

Dietz, Mary. 1983. *Killing for profit.* Chicago: Nelson-Hall.

Douglas, Jack. 1967. *The social meanings of suicide.* Princeton, N.J.: Princeton University Press.

Driver, Edwin. 1961. Interaction and criminal homicide in India. *Social Forces* 40:153–58.

Erickson, Kai. 1966. *Wayward puritans: A study in the sociology of deviance.* New York: Wiley.

Erlanger, Howard. 1974. The empirical status of the subculture of violence thesis. *Social Problems* 22:280–92.

Ferracuti, Franco, Renato Lazzari, and Marvin Wolfgang. 1970. *Violence in Sardinia.* Rome: Bulzoni.

Ferracuti, Franco, and Graeme Newman. 1974. Assaultive offenses. In *Handbook of criminology,* ed. D. Glaser, 175–207. Chicago: Rand McNally.

Ferracuti, Franco, and Marvin Wolfgang. 1963. Design for a proposed study of violence. *British Journal of Criminology* 3:377–88.

———. 1964. The prediction of violent behavior. *Corrective Psychiatry and Journal of Social Therapy* 10: 289–301.

———. 1973. *Psychological testing of the subculture of violence.* Rome: Bulzoni.

Finestone, Harold. 1976. *Victims of change: Juvenile delinquents in American society.* Westport, Conn.: Greenwood.

Fisher, Gary. 1970. Discriminating violence emanating from overcontrolled versus under-controlled aggressivity. *British Journal of Social and Clinical Psychology* 9:54–59.

Fisher, Gary, and Ephraim Rivlin. 1971. Psychological needs of rapists. *British Journal of Criminology* 11:182–85.

Glaser, Daniel. 1956. Criminality theories and behavioral images. *American Journal of Sociology* 61:433–44.

Gould, Stephen. 1983 [1981]. *The mismeasure of man.* New York: Norton.

Harlan, Howard. 1950. Five hundred homicides. *Journal of Criminal Law and Criminology* 40:736–52.

Hartung, Frank. 1966. *Crime, law and society.* Detroit: Wayne State University Press.

Hayek, Frederick. 1952. *The counter-revolution of science.* New York: Free Press.

Hepburn, John, and Harwin Voss. 1970. Patterns of criminal homicide: A comparison of Chicago and Philadelphia. *Criminology* 8:21–45.

Hughes, Evert. 1937. Institutional office and the person. *American Journal of Sociology* 43:404–13.

———. 1962. What other? In *Human behavior and social processes,* ed. A. Rose, 119–27. Boston: Houghton Mifflin.

Jacoby, Russell. 1987. *The last intellectuals.* New York: Noonday.

Jeffery, C. Ray. 1960. The historical development of criminology. In *Pioneers in criminology,* ed. H. Mannheim, 364–94. Chicago: Quadrangle.

Johnson, John. 1975. *Doing field research.* New York: Free Press.

Justice, Blair, and Roger Birkman. 1972. An effort to distinguish the violent from the nonviolent. *Southern Medical Journal* 65:703–06.

Katz, Jack. 1988. *Seductions of crime.* New York: Basic.

Kitsuse, John, and Aaron Cicourel. 1963. A note on the uses of official statistics. *Social Problems* 12:131–39.

Landua, Simha, Israel Drapkin, and Shlomo Arad. 1974. Homicide victims and offenders: An Israeli study. *Journal of Criminal Law and Criminology* 65:390–96.

Lejeune, Robert. 1981. Review of L. Athens's *Violent criminal acts and actors. The Sociological Review* 29:155–57.

Lester, David, and Gene Lester. 1975. *Crime of passion: Murder and murderer.* Chicago: Nelson-Hall.

Lester, David, and William Perdue. 1973. Movement responses of murderers to Rorschach stimuli. *Perceptual and Motor Skills* 37:668.

Lester, David, William Perdue, and David Brookhart. 1974. Murder and the control of aggression. *Psychological Reports* 34:706.

Levy, Jerrold, Stephen Kunitz, and Michael Everett. 1969. Navajo criminal homicide. *Southwestern Journal of Anthropology* 25:124–52.

Lilly, Robert, Francis Cullen, and Richard Ball. 1995. *Criminological theory.* Thousand Oaks, Calif.: Sage.

Lindesmith, Alfred. 1968. *Addiction and opiates.* Chicago: Aldine.

———. 1981. Symbolic interactionism and causality. *Symbolic Interaction* 4:87–96.

Luckenbill, David. 1977. Criminal homicide as a situated transaction. *Social Problems* 25:176–86.

Lundsgaarde, Henry. 1981. Review of L. Athens's *Violent criminal acts and actors. Newsletter of the Association for Political and Legal Anthropology* 5:12–16.

MacDonald, John. 1971. *Rape: Offenders and their victims.* Springfield, Ill.: Charles Thomas.

Mallory, Charles, and C. Eugene Walker. 1972. MMPI O-H scale responses of assaultive and nonassaultive prisoners and associated life history variables. *Educational and Psychological Measurement* 32:1125–28.

Matza, David. 1964. *Delinquency and drift.* New York: Wiley.

McCreary, Charles. 1976. Trait and type differences among male and female assaultive and non-assaultive offenders. *Journal of Personality Assessment* 40:617–21.

McKenzie, Roderick. 1971 [1924]. The ecological approach to the study of the human ecology. In *The social fabric of the metropolis: Contributions of the Chicago school of urban sociology,* ed. J. Short, 17–32. Chicago: University of Chicago Press.

Mead, George. 1932. *The philosophy of the present.* LaSalle, Ill.: Open Court.

———. 1934. *Mind, self and society.* Chicago: University of Chicago Press.

———. 1936. *Movements of thought in the nineteenth century.* Chicago: University of Chicago Press.

———. 1964. *Selected writings.* Ed. A. Reck. Indianapolis: Bobbs-Merril.

Megargee, Edwin. 1965. Assault with intent to kill. *Transaction* 2:27–31.

———. 1966. Undercontrolled and overcontrolled personality types in extreme antisocial aggression. *Psychological Monographs: General and Applied* 80:1–29.

———. 1973. Recent research on overcontrolled and undercontrolled personality patterns among violent offenders. *Sociological Symposium* 9:37–50.

———. 1982. Psychological determinants and correlates of criminal violence. In *Criminal violence,* ed. M. Wolfgang and N. Weiner, 81–170. Beverly Hills, Calif.: Sage.

Megargee, Edwin, and Patrick Cook. 1967. The relation of T.A.T. and inkblot aggressive content scales with each other and with criteria of overt aggressiveness in juvenile delinquents. *Journal of Projective Techniques and Personality Assessment* 31:48–60.

Megargee, Edwin, Patrick Cook, and Gerald Mendelsohn. 1967. Development and validation of an MMPI scale of assaultiveness in overcontrolled individuals. *Journal of Abnormal Psychology* 72:519–23.

Megargee, Edwin, and Gerald Mendelsohn. 1962. A cross-validation of twelve MMPI indices of hostility and control. *Journal of Abnormal and Social Psychology* 65:431–38.

Miller, David. 1973. *George Herbert Mead: Self, language and the world.* Austin: University of Texas Press.

Mills, C. Wright. 1943. The professional ideology of social pathologists. *American Journal of Sociology* 49:165–80.

———. 1959. *The sociological imagination.* New York: Oxford University Press.

———. 1963. *Power, politics and people: The collected essays of C. Wright Mills.* Ed. I. Horowitz. New York: Oxford University Press.

Moore, Mark, Susan Estrich, Daniel McGillis, and William Spelmon. 1984. *Dangerous offenders: The elusive target of justice.* Boston: Harvard University Press.

Mulvihill, Donald, and Melvin Tumin with Lynn Curtis. 1969. *Crimes of violence (a staff report to the National Commission on the Causes and*

Prevention of Violence), vol. 11. Washington, D.C.: U.S. Government Printing Office.

Newman, Graeme. 1980. Review of L. Athens's *Violent criminal acts and actors. The Annals of the American Academy of Political and Social Sciences* 450:288–89.

Park, Robert. 1938. Reflections on communication and culture. *American Journal of Sociology* 44:187–205.

———. 1952. *Human communities.* New York: Free Press.

———. 1967. *On social control and collective behavior: Selected papers.* Ed. R. Turner. Chicago: University of Chicago Press.

Park, Robert, and Ernest Burgess. *Introduction to the science of sociology.* 1969 [1924]. Chicago: University of Chicago Press.

Perdue, William, and David Lester. 1972. Personality characteristics of rapists. *Perceptual and Motor Skills* 35:514.

———. 1974. Racial differences in the personality of murderers. *Perceptual and Motor Skills* 38:726.

Persons, Roy, and Philip Marks. 1971. The violent 4-3 MMPI personality type. *Journal of Consulting and Clinical Psychology* 36:189–96.

Pittman, David, and William Handy. 1964. Patterns in criminal aggravated assault. *Journal of Criminal Law, Criminology and Police Science* 55:462–70.

Pokorny, Alex. 1965a. A comparison of homicides in two cities. *Journal of Criminal Law, Criminology and Police Science* 56:479–87.

———. 1965b. Human violence: A comparison of homicide, aggravated assault, suicide and attempted suicide. *Journal of Criminal Law, Criminology and Police Science* 56:488–97.

Rader, Charles. 1977. MMPI profile types of exposers, rapists, and assaulters in a court services population. *Journal of Consulting and Clinical Psychology* 45:61–69.

Rawlins, Mark. 1973. Self-control and interpersonal violence: A study of Scottish adolescent male severe offenders. *Criminology* 11:23–48.

Ray, Melvin, and Ray Simmons. 1987. Convicted murderers' accounts of their crimes: A study of homicide in small communities. *Symbolic Interaction* 10:57–70.

Sarbin, Theodore, and Ernst Wenk. 1969. Resolution of binocular rivalry as a means of identifying violence-prone offenders. *Journal of Criminal Law, Criminology and Police Science* 60:345–50.

Sarbin, Theodore, Ernst Wenk, and David Sherwood. 1968. An effort to identify assault-prone offenders. *Journal of Research in Crime and Delinquency* 5:66–71.

Schutz, Alfred. 1954. Concept and theory formation in the social sciences. *Journal of Philosophy* 51:257–73.

Sellin, Thorsten. 1938. *Culture conflict and crime*. New York: Social Science Research Council.

Shibutani, Tamotsu. 1955. Reference groups as perspectives. *American Journal of Sociology* 60:562–69.

———. 1970. On the personification of adversaries. In *Human nature and collective behavior*, ed. T. Shibutani, 223–33. Englewood Cliffs, N.J.: Prentice-Hall.

Stark, Rodney, and James McEvoy III. 1970. Middle-class violence. *Psychology Today* 4:52–54, 110–12.

Sutherland, Edwin. 1973. *On analyzing crime*. Ed. K. Schuessler. Chicago: University of Chicago Press.

Sutherland, Edwin, and Donald Cressey. 1978. *Criminology*. Philadelphia: Lippincott.

Svalastoga, Kaare. 1956. Homicide and social contact in Denmark. *American Journal of Sociology* 62:37–41.

———. 1962. Rape and social structure. *Pacific Sociological Review* 5:48–53.

Tanay, Emanuel. 1972. Psychiatric aspects of homicide prevention. *American Journal of Psychiatry* 128:49–52.

Taylor, Ian, Paul Walton, and Jock Young. 1973. *The new criminology: For a social theory of deviance*. New York: Harper and Row.

Thomas, William I. 1967 [1923]. *The unadjusted girl*. New York: Harper and Row.

Toch, Hans. 1969. *Violent men: An inquiry into the psychology of violence*. Chicago: Aldine.

Townsend, Kim. 1987. *Sherwood Anderson*. Boston: Houghton Mifflin.

Valentine, People vs. 28 Cal. 2d 121, 169 P. 2d 1 (1946).

Vold, George. 1958. *Theoretical criminology*. New York: Oxford University Press.

Vold, George, and Thomas Bernard. 1986. *Theoretical criminology*. New York: Oxford University Press.

Voss, Harwin, and John Hepburn. 1968. Patterns of criminal homicide in Chicago. *Journal of Criminal Law, Criminology and Police Science* 59:499–508.

Wagner, Edwin, and Roger Hawkins. 1964. Differentiation of assaultive delinquents with the hand test. *Journal of Projective Techniques and Personality Assessment* 28:363–65.

Wallace, Samuel. 1964. Patterns of violence in San Juan. In *Interdisciplinary problems in criminology: Papers of the American Society of Criminology*, 43–48. Columbus: Ohio State University Publication.

Warder, John. 1969. Two studies of violent offenders. *British Journal of Criminology* 9:389–93.

Wenk, Ernst, Theodore Sarbin, and David Sherwood. 1968. The resolution of binocular rivalry among assaultive and nonassaultive youthful offenders. *Journal of Research in Crime and Delinquency* 5:134–47.

Williams, Frank, and Marilyn McShane. 1994. *Criminological theory.* Englewood Cliffs, N.J.: Prentice-Hall.

Winch, Peter. 1958. *The idea of a social science.* London: Routledge and Kegan Paul.

Wirth, Louis. 1928. *The ghetto.* Chicago: University of Chicago Press.

Wolfe, Thomas. 1936. *The story of a novel.* New York: Scribner's.

Wolfgang, Marvin. 1957. Victim-precipitated criminal homicide. *Journal of Criminal Law, Criminology and Police Science* 48:1–11.

———. 1958. *Patterns of criminal homicide.* Philadelphia: University of Pennsylvania Press.

———. 1967. Criminal homicide and the subculture of violence. In *Studies in homicide,* ed. M. Wolfgang, 3–12. New York: Harper and Row.

———. 1968. Homicide. In *International encyclopedia of the social sciences,* ed. David Sills, 3:490–95. New York: Macmillan/Free Press.

———. 1969. Who kills whom. *Psychology Today* 3:54–56, 72, 74–75.

Wolfgang, Marvin and Franco Ferracuti. 1967a. *The subculture of violence: Towards an integrated theory in criminology.* London: Tavistock.

———. 1967b. Subculture of violence—a social psychological theory. In *Studies in homicide,* ed. M. Wolfgang, 271–80. New York: Harper and Row.

Znaniecki, Florian. 1968 [1934]. *The method of sociology.* New York: Octagon.

Index

LONNIE ATHENS, who received his doctorate in criminology from the University of California at Berkeley, has studied violent criminals for twenty-five years, served as a consultant on numerous capital murder cases, and published an earlier book, *The Creation of Dangerous Violent Criminals*. He was senior research criminologist at Georgetown University Law Center and is now an associate professor in the criminal justice department at Seton Hall University.

UNIVERSITY OF ILLINOIS PRESS
1325 SOUTH OAK STREET
CHAMPAIGN, ILLINOIS 61820-6903
WWW.PRESS.UILLINOIS.EDU